SIMPLE
ACTS
of
KINDNESS

SIMPLE
ACTS
of
KINDNESS

PRACTICAL WAYS TO HELP

PEOPLE IN NEED

TERRI GREEN

Fleming H. Revell
A Division of Baker Book House Co
Grand Rapids, Michigan 49516

Published by Fleming H. Revell
a division of Baker Book House Company
P.O. Box 6287, Grand Rapids, MI 49516-6287
www.bakerbooks.com

Printed in the United States of America

Library of Congress Cataloging-in-Publication Data
Green, Terri.
    Simple acts of kindness : practical ways to help people in need / Terri Green.
        p.   cm.
    ISBN 0-8007-5879-X (pbk.)
    1. Helping behavior—Religious aspects—Christianity. 2. Kindness—Religious aspects—Christianity. I. Title.
    BV4647.H4G74 2004
    241'.4—dc22   2003020015

To Brad, Kara, Tayler, and Paige,
Your lives inspire so many.
To Dad,
Your short life gave me a chance to know God's grace.

CONTENTS

FOREWORD

Over the years many aspiring writers have come to me for help with writing a book. I don't know if it was my poor advice or their loss of motivation, but only two people that I know of went on to write and to be published. One is Leesa Bellesi, who wrote *The Kingdom Assignment* that was featured on *Oprah*. The other is my friend Terri Green, whose book you are holding in your hands. When Terri expressed an interest in writing, I wanted to help her because I knew she had something to say. With her delightful humor and bright intellect, I felt certain she could write. My only concern was how she would find the time. She is raising three girls, her oldest with severe cerebral palsy. Terri works outside of her home, exercises most every day, and stays active in the church. Despite all of that, she found the time to write and to write well.

I have known Terri and her family for over twenty years and have walked with them through many tough moments. I have always marveled at what an amazing, nurturing, and skilled mother Terri is. I want my daughter Madeline to be like her girls. I want to parent Madeline the way she and Brad are parenting their kids. Terri has consistently proven to be a godly woman and a mother that I greatly admire.

Books like this one are often written from lofty towers by writers who can only imagine what it would be like to live through hard times and dark hours. This book is different because Terri and Brad have lived through many trials that would have left other lives broken. I have watched these two climb out of the pit of hopelessness to a place of honor and stability. During their darkest moments they were shown love, support, and comfort. Many kind gestures and countless prayers from others kept them going. Once they came out of their deep despair, they went on to help others in similar situations. They transformed their pain into a new purpose and began to help other hurting people the way God had helped them. That transformation is the foundation of this book.

If you are going through a tragedy, heartache, financial despair, or even the loss of a loved one, this book will encourage you to persevere. Read it all the way through to the end. You will see that God loves you and cares for you in the midst of this very tough time. If you have experienced any of these hardships, *Simple Acts of Kindness* will inspire you to rise up after the dust has settled and help others through their struggles. It will cause you to create a "Do unto others" lifestyle for yourself and will change the meaning and purpose of your life.

Stephen Arterburn

ACKNOWLEDGMENTS

This book was inspired by the gift of giving that many people showed our family through their simple acts of kindness. Several people are named throughout the following chapters, but thoses whose names are not written down will never be forgotten.

The following pages are dedicated to all of you for the limitless ways you have displayed God's love to our family and to others. It is the great testimony of your character and your gifts that gave us the idea to help others who are hurting. The unconditional love conveyed by all of you helped pull us through many dark moments. On behalf of my family and me, thank you from the bottom of my heart.

Special thanks to the endorsers of this book. It would not have been published without you. To Rick and Kay, you are without a doubt the most inspirational people Brad and I know. To Pastor Greg, your message introduced me to Christ at the age of seventeen, and I will always be grateful to you. To Joni, your encouragement and advice have been invaluable to me. To Colleen, your energy and playfulness are refreshing. I am especially grateful for our friendship. To Anthony and Dee Dee

Munoz, your lives have been amazing to watch—we miss you. To Kathleen, you are an incredible woman. I don't know how you keep it all together and still raise a child like mine. To Irene Black-Dunlap, congratulations on the Chicken Soup for the Soul books. I am thrilled with your success and I thank you for your support. Above all, thank you, Stephen. I can't express in words how much we value our many years of friendship with you. I can't wait to see how God unfolds the rest of our lives.

Stephen, you introduced me to Alive Communications where I met the best agents in the world (Lee, you are the greatest). You sang my praises to Linda Glasford, who introduced me to Jennifer of Baker Books/Revell. Thank you, Linda, Greg, and Lee, for giving me a chance.

Thank you to Jennifer, Karen, Twila, Mary, and the rest of the Revell team for believing in me. Thank you, Carol, for the love of your red pencil and for the existence of our true-blue friendship. Thank you to Rob, Sharon, and the rest of the associates for indulging me and keeping me employed while I ride this wave. Thank you to my girl friends and others for your faithful friendship and encouragement all the way through (you know who you are). Finally, thank you to all of Brad's family who have been a source of comfort and support. And to my family, even though you are miles away, I have never felt closer to you.

May the God of hope fill you with all joy and peace as you trust in him, so that you may overflow with hope by the power of the Holy Spirit.

Romans 15:13

INTRODUCTION

As Jesus was sending out his twelve disciples to preach the Good News and to heal, among the instructions he gave them was a brief command that spoke volumes: "Freely you have received, freely give" (Matt. 10:8).

My family and I have been the recipients of many gifts of love and kindness, time and meals, and several other amazing gestures from people who simply have a caring heart and an eagerness to help someone in need. Because of their example, I'm eager to give back to someone else who needs help. One of the ways I hope to do that is through writing this book.

For more than twelve years, I've shared our story with large and small audiences. When someone would suggest that I write a book about our experiences, I considered that idea for only a few seconds before dismissing it. All that changed in May 1999 when I shared my testimony with the congregation of Saddleback Valley Community Church in Lake Forest, California, at the request of Pastor Rick Warren.

That weekend I spoke to approximately fourteen thousand people over five different services. After that overwhelming experience, I realized I was trying to convey something different to the audiences. This time I was telling more than the story of my girls' lives and how it impacted my life. During my message I acknowledged several people who had done kind, caring, and amazing things for Brad and me while we struggled through one tragedy after another. At this point I felt an inspiration to write our story and to honor those people who heeded the advice of their Lord and Savior, Jesus Christ, and gave themselves freely to others.

Our Story

My husband, Brad, and I dated for three years prior to our marriage. During our courtship, my father was ill and almost bedridden. We thought we were going through the toughest part of our lives, but this hardship and its sadness were really preparing us for many rough years ahead.

We were married just weeks after my father died in 1980. Although we had planned the wedding so that my father could attend, God took him before it could take place. My dad was forty-five years young, just a couple of years older than I am now.

After we were married, Brad and I discussed having children. He wanted to have them and I didn't—it was that simple.

We were married for four years when, unexpectedly, I became pregnant with our first daughter. The pregnancy itself prepared me for motherhood and calmed some of my fears—even then I began to feel a love for my child whom I had yet to see.

Our daughter Kara was born two months prematurely. The doctors immediately said that she had a cardiac condition that could possibly require surgery in a year or so. But when she was ten days old and still in the hospital, she went into congestive heart failure and needed emergency surgery. She successfully survived the operation, but many complications followed. After a two-month stay in the intensive care unit, she was released to us with a long list of instructions and sad suggestions. The evening before we were to introduce her to her newly decorated nursery in our little condo, the chief neonatal unit physician sat me down and said that Kara's hearing test showed she would eventually be deaf, her brain scan showed she would be in a vegetative state all her life, and her heart anomalies were so severe that she would not live past the age of five. Then he suggested that we seriously consider institutionalizing our tiny baby. Brad and I both felt that she was a gift to us from God. We were sure he would give us the strength to care for her ourselves.

In her first four years of life, Kara underwent fourteen surgeries on various parts of her body. Then when she was in a somewhat stable condition, the doctors encouraged us to have a sibling for her. They said it would be good for all of us to have a healthy son or daughter in our home. They assured us that none of Kara's anomalies were genetic and said the chance that we would have a second child with disabilities was incredibly slim.

We planned our second daughter, Tayler. She was born just two weeks before her due date, and she was a beautiful bundle of joy. When the nurses brought her into my hospital room, they had her right arm in a sling. "She broke her collarbone while she descended through the birth canal," they explained.

Brad and I weren't very concerned. "A broken bone can heal," we said to comfort each other. But Tayler showed signs of difficulty immediately. She wasn't interested in nursing or drinking from a bottle, and the nurses began to send me over the edge. They brought me La Leche League videos and booklets on how to properly breast-feed a baby. My hospital experience was beginning to feel like a prison sentence.

Our family's pediatrician, who we felt saved Kara's life, wanted us to have a normal hospital experience this time. He suggested that we take Tayler home and call him in the morning with her progress. That's just what we did. The following morning I phoned to give him a progress report. After a short conversation, he instructed me to return our newborn to the hospital for testing. Tayler had started to nurse just a little bit while she was at home with us, and she had a sort of bowel movement, which was what the doctor was hoping to hear. But she also started to vomit up a green substance.

The results of Tayler's testing called for emergency surgery on her intestine. She was born with a twisted small bowel, called a malrotation. Half of her small intestine had died in utero, and the dead intestine had to be removed. The remaining sections would have to heal before the doctors could attempt to reconnect the incomplete bowel.

Two weeks and two operations later, Tayler was dying. They told us she was no longer able to fight off an infection caused by the high-risk surgeries. I'll never forget the expression on the nurse's face when she said that they were ready to disconnect the life support and allow Tayler to die in my arms.

With a visiting pastor, the surgeon, a few nurses, and Brad's parents already standing at Tayler's crib, we prayed in the ICU. For hours before our prayer and during the prayer itself, Tayler's body lay still. Immediately after the last amen was uttered, Tayler moved. Her movement was somewhat like a sigh, and I felt it was a sign that Tayler was going to live.

The days that followed were a blur, but we knew that Tayler was the recipient of a modern-day miracle. All of the doctors admitted that there was nothing they could have done to save her. They actually said that she was completely in God's hands.

Six months and five operations later, Tayler was released from the hospital. She came home with a feeding tube, an IV line, and sixteen-hour-a-day nursing care. But the amazing thing is that she came home at all.

Once Tayler was home, we had quite a busy household. Kara had a feeding tube as well because of her "failure to thrive" syndrome—she simply didn't want to eat. We were medically involved but emotionally numb.

We were done making babies, so we thought. We were using everything short of a chastity belt for protection, but I got pregnant again. Because we were sure this baby too would have some kind of physical, medical, or developmental crisis, we were emotional wrecks.

During this third pregnancy I was restricted to bed rest for seven months with placenta abruptia, a condition in which the placenta separates from the wall of the uterus and causes bleeding. Thankfully, state resources and our medical insurance company allowed us to hire nursing care for our first two girls. Our help would even throw in a load of laundry and put on a pot of spaghetti in the same visit!

At almost full term, our darling little Paige was born by cesarean section. Immediately after X-rays and other testing, the doctors assured us that she was completely healthy. We took her home when she was five days old and waited patiently for the other shoe to drop.

We were home with her for less than a week when our faithful pediatrician called and said that there had been a mistake

19

when the radiologist read the X-rays taken at Paige's birth. He said there was a misdistribution of air in her intestine and that we needed to rush her to the hospital for further testing.

I could have driven to that hospital blindfolded. When we arrived, the technicians and radiologist were waiting to test her without delay. I sat in the lobby for what felt like days, filling out the paperwork that I had memorized. Then the nurses handed my baby back to me.

With Paige in my arms, I slowly walked down the long, cold hospital corridor to go home and await the phone call that would explain the doctor's next course of action. When I heard my name being called from a distance behind us, I turned around to see the radiologist himself walking rapidly toward Paige and me. I had never directly talked to him, but I could have used his invoices to wallpaper a small room. He said, "You probably don't know me, but my name is Dr. Smith, and I know your other two girls. I just want you to know that this baby is fine." I felt as if an angel had just spoken to me. I could only imagine what this doctor must have been thinking. I will never forget his words or his kind intentions to save me from any more moments of distress.

Today Kara is nineteen years old. She has had twenty-three surgeries and procedures, but only three heart surgeries. Her cardiologist now sees her on a biannual basis. Her hearing is not perfect, but she is not deaf. She doesn't speak, but she communicates just the same. She uses a wheelchair to get around, and she is a far cry from being in a vegetative state! She attends a local high school in Southern California, enrolled in their special education department. She is the best friend anyone could have.

Tayler is fifteen years old. She only has the physical scars and very few side effects left from her traumatic beginning. She was totally healed by God. It's an amazing feeling to have a living miracle in our home. She is a beautiful girl and an aspiring actress. Brad and I are awestruck when she performs on the stage in musical theater. She is a straight A student, and she has tremendous compassion for her older sister and others like Kara. She is always eager to help me with any of Kara's needs.

Paige is thirteen years old now. She is the smartest of us all. She loves to write and play music, and she has learned to play four instruments already. She too is a straight A student enrolled in honors classes. Paige brought normalcy to our family. She has a quirky sense of humor, and she professes that she wants to become a surgeon when she grows up. Other than eight months of colic (which seemed like eight years), Paige was and is completely fine.

Living through my father's illness and eventually his death, we were more prepared to call on the strength we would need to live through our children's difficult conditions. Without a doubt, it was God's grace and the acts of kindness from others that held our marriage together, saved us from financial ruin, and made us believe that even in the worst of situations there is goodness all around us. Every kind deed from others was another hug from God, assuring us that everything was going to be all right. "Trust me," he was saying to our hearts. And so we did. I hope this book will inspire you to reach out to those who are in need.

Do not be anxious about anything, but in everything, by prayer and petition, with thanksgiving, present your requests to God. And the peace of God, which transcends all understanding, will guard your hearts and your minds in Christ Jesus.

Philippians 4:6–7

PART 1

GIVE YOURSELF
TO OTHERS—
GOD WILL HELP

1

LEND ME YOUR EARS

I wish I had a nickel for every moment that I needed someone to just hear me out. I had enough professionals giving me advice about what to do for Kara and for Tayler. I needed somebody to hear my cries and not reply with what they thought I should do. No advice, just understanding.

One of those somebodies for me during so many dark days and rough times was my good friend Debe. Debe has given me and my family amazing help during our difficult times. But I appreciated her listening ear most of all. It was and still is the one thing that seems hard for most people to do. She would listen and comfort me when I cried. All of my friends have become like family to me through our hard times. We have listened to each other in the worst of situations. But Debe was in the thick of it with me from day one.

Debe and I became pregnant within six months of each other. My baby was due first. We grew big together with our pregnancies, then she supported me every minute once Kara was born.

She always put aside her feelings and would ask me first how I was doing. I'd have to catch myself in the middle of my moaning and turn the conversation around to inquire, "Oh, I'm sorry, how are you?" She felt that whatever her situation was, it was minor in comparison to mine, and so she put the world into perspective for herself.

I have to admit that I have fallen into the category of unso-

THOUGHTFUL SUGGESTIONS

1. None of us will escape having a lousy day now and then. Put your difficult day aside and try to comfort your friend or loved one. His rough day may top yours.
2. Don't try to put a Band-Aid on your friend's hardship. Sometimes it just compounds her issues. If you haven't been in her shoes, she may only be discouraged and confused by your unsolicited advice.
3. Even if you are older (and possibly wiser), remember that you are not living in the other person's situation. You may have knowledge and experience of another kind, to be reserved for another time. Advice from a truly familiar friend is easy to hear, but mere words to fill an uncomfortable silence can be deafening. And unbroken silence can feel like nonacceptance. Be careful with what you say.
4. If you don't know how to comfort friends, then simply tell them the truth, "I am so sorry, I don't know what to tell you. I just don't know what to say." Then a physical hug if their body language calls for it may be all the conversation that is needed for the moment.

licited advisor to some of my friends at one time or another. I'm embarrassed to realize that the listeners may have hung up the phone and just rolled their eyes. Who can blame them? Being a listening friend is like being someone's human journal. The journal never speaks back to you. It accepts every word that you write, unconditionally. A journal gives you the opportunity to vent without being criticized. Wouldn't it be nice to know that you are thought of as a person who can be trusted not to judge someone by their thoughts or by their hardships? "Friends, Romans, countrymen, lend me your ears." Notice that Mark Antony didn't ask his audience to lend him advice.

> Do not be quick with your mouth,
>   do not be hasty in your heart
>   to utter anything before God.
> God is in heaven
>   and you are on earth,
>   so let your words be few.

> Ecclesiastes 5:2

2

WHAT'S MINE IS YOURS

It was the Christmas season of 1990. We had three girls in diapers, and two of them had gastrostomy (feeding) tubes. Brad had joined the Newport Beach Police Department and had started his training. He was virtually gone to the police academy for five months, and he had shaved his head almost bald. I was jealous. Oh, not because he could have a bald head and I couldn't, but because he could have some long-term respite from feeding tubes and diapers. He was enrolled November 30, so the holiday merriment would be completely my responsibility. It was a depressing thought.

I was not feeling the Christmas spirit, nor was I ready to bring in a New Year of the same routine. All I wanted for Christmas was a nervous breakdown. I would picture it; the green grass, white padded walls with clean tile floors, and every meal prepared just for me. I would have a new white outfit to wear. (I looked

29

good in white. It went well with my usually hidden-from-the-sun complexion.) My arms are double-jointed, so the funny little sleeves in the jacket of my new getup that would wrap around my body would probably even be comfortable for me, or at least it would give me that "I really love myself" look. Most of all, the place would be peaceful and quiet.

That Christmas many people anonymously left gifts on our doorstep. They knew it would embarrass me to be given gifts for our girls when we couldn't reciprocate at all. One evening the bell rang, and before I could approach the door, the giver was gone. Sitting on the porch was a basket of gifts for the girls and a tiny little box that was addressed to me. I closed the door and placed the gifts for the girls under our sorry little tree, but I was much too curious to set down the petite package that bore my name.

I unwrapped the gift quickly, and inside the parcel was a pair of beautiful sapphire earrings. The earrings were not new, so that aroused my suspicions about the note that was also enclosed. The note read something like this:

> "These earrings were worn by a mother of a child with a handi-cap. She would like you to have them now. Merry Christmas, with love . . ."

At the bottom of the note was a Scripture verse, Jeremiah 29:11. The note said that this verse was especially for me. I looked it up in my Bible, and it read:

> "For I know the plans I have for you," declares the LORD, "plans to prosper you and not to harm you, plans to give you hope and a future."

Immediately I thought that this woman couldn't be familiar with me. She must not have really known how devastated we were financially or how much work it was for me to care for these three tiny girls, especially the two with special needs. Paige had colic at that point, and it was making me nuts.

To accept the earrings meant that I would also have to receive and believe in the words of the Scripture on the note. I wasn't ready to do that yet because I had no hope. I was convinced that the future plans for me were bleak at best. And I was sure that the next shoe would drop, and when it did, it would drop fast and hard. I put the box with the note and the earrings away in a safe place. But I never forgot they were there.

As time went by, I realized that I had been relying on my own strength and energy to survive my situation. I wasn't looking past my circumstances each day. I was banking on what had happened and not optimistically looking forward to what could happen.

Some years passed, and it became clear to me that I had a tendency to read the Bible and apply only some of its principles to my life. Eventually it also became clear to me that if I rejected part of the Bible that way, I would have to reject all of it. The promise of a future and a hope had to apply to all people who believe in Christ as their Savior, and since I did believe in him, I needed to believe that there was hope and a future for me too. His plans for my future are sometimes unclear to me still, but I now know that I can be content in whatever circumstances come my way. In that, I have great hope.

Because of their significance, the earrings that I once rejected I wear often now. I don't wear them every day for fear I'll lose them. But every time I wear them, I feel a confidence

THOUGHTFUL SUGGESTIONS

1. Give away a piece of jewelry that you can part with and that you believe the recipient will appreciate.
2. Give away a book that was an inspiration to you. You can share with the recipient a page or a chapter that spoke to you in hard times.
3. You may have received a gift that has a story behind it. A doll, a stuffed animal, a scarf, a piece of clothing that is almost like new. Share the story of the special giver with your friend or loved one.
4. You may be surprised that what you have may be of comfort to someone who is hurting. Look around you. Make whatever you give shine like a new copper penny. Maybe the gift *is* a new penny or a coin with a story. Present it in the best condition possible and be proud of your gift. After all, it's coming from your heart.

in Christ that nothing will shake my faith again to the point of feeling the need for a new white outfit sporting wraparound sleeves.

The next time you are befuddled over what to do for the person in your life who is hurting, think hard and use your imagination. What do you have that this person would appreciate, and what words would leave a lasting impression on her for the circumstances that she is facing in hard times? Do you have something that you can part with that would cost you virtually nothing? Give it with a note of encouragement that is relevant to the person who is hurting. The impact can last a lifetime.

Remember that with this act of giving, it's the words that count the most. It doesn't have to cost you anything to help someone else. The cost is the loss of an heirloom or object that you no longer make use of yourself. The memory of giving something away that has a special meaning will also last *you* a lifetime.

For where your treasure is, there your heart will be also.

Luke 12:34

3

IN GOD WE TRUST

I t is incredibly humbling to admit that we were ever in a position to accept money from anyone other than an employer. We never asked for it and many times we refused it, but in desperate times we accepted it. The following stories are just a couple of ways in which we were blessed by very selfless people in the act of giving.

Kara was just an infant, and we were living in our first tiny condo in Lake Forest, California. She was equipped with a feeding tube, heart monitors, seizure medication, heart medication, a hearing device, and ear tubes. Brad had just arrived home from work one evening when he heard the doorbell. He opened the front door to find a young boy maybe seven years old standing on the porch holding an envelope. No car waiting outside, no bicycle leaning up against the wall, just the boy and this envelope. He said to Brad, "Someone asked me to give this envelope to you." Brad asked who had sent him, and the boy said he didn't know. Brad accepted the envelope, thanked the young man, and closed the door. Then he told me about our little visitor. I ran to the balcony to see if I knew the boy, but he was nowhere in sight. We heard no running feet, no car drive off, and no skidding bicycle tires. We opened the envelope and discovered a $100 bill inside. We had only God to thank.

After having both Kara and Tayler, we tried to maintain a good-standing relationship with the twelve medical specialists whom our girls saw for treatment. We used our credit cards to pay the balances that our medical insurance would not cover. I use the words "credit cards," plural, because once we filled one card to its maximum, we would apply for another, then another and another. We realize now that our strategy was not the greatest, but we felt that bankruptcy was not an option for us. Borrowing money from anyone else was also out of the question in our minds.

Every year we made a new plan to pay off a credit card. We teased that we would have to start making homemade gasoline to fuel our cars or some fool thing like that to save money. It all seemed so hopeless. (Just for the record, we never resorted to making homemade gasoline.) But our real plans were just as futile. They never got us out of debt.

Then one day we decided to take the plunge. We decided to trust God with our money. We had always agreed that every time a pastor gave a tithing message at church, we felt there was an underlying plea: "We need your money more than you do." But we eventually realized what they were really saying: "God doesn't need your money, but *you* need to give your money to him. Just watch what he will do for you when you trust him with it."

That brought us into a quandary—do we tithe on the net or do we tithe on the gross? Our friend Melinda gave us great advice with her counter question, "Do you want to be blessed on the net or do you want to be blessed on the gross?"

I remember it like it was yesterday. It was in March 1995 that we took a step of faith and made a commitment to really trust God with our money. After we wrote our first tithe check to the church, we prayed and asked that God would feed us and make the rest of our weeks between paychecks livable. But what if something even more catastrophic were to happen? What,

THOUGHTFUL SUGGESTIONS

1. Give money anonymously, but safely. Send an envelope of cash with a messenger that you trust, someone like the boy who graced our doorstep. Have a cashier's check made up at the bank and address it to the recipient. Send it by registered mail in a sealed, opaque envelope. Include a return address that the receiver will not recognize, but one that you have made arrangements with just in case it is returned. If possible, research a debt that the person or family owes and directly make a payment to that account. Ask for a receipt for your own records.

2. If you have a relationship with a church or a tax-exempt organization that is willing to receive a donation from you and pass on a portion or the entire gift to the family, this will make it possible for you to have a tax-deductible receipt for your offering to a friend.

3. Hand your friend a card that expresses the pain you feel while watching what he is going through. Include a check or cash and explain that it will help you with your own grief for him if he would be willing to receive a gift from you.

where, when, and how were the first words out of our mouths each day.

We never went hungry, our kids always had shoes on their feet, and believe it or not, no more financial catastrophes took place.

Then just two months later, Brad's parents generously gave us a portion of an inheritance that was given to Brad's dad. It was such a large amount of money that it paid off two of our credit cards and then some. We are forever grateful. We never asked them for it; they just gave as God directed them to give.

Have you been blessed with the financial means to help someone else who is currently struggling to make ends meet? Money is not always the perfect gift. It was the hardest gift for us to receive. Like us, most people want to be able to financially provide for their own family. It involves a sense of pride. Be careful when you offer a gift of money. The reason for anonymity is simply this: There is no way for the recipient to reject the gift. If you are not giving anonymously, remind your friends that life has its time of famine and its time of harvest. Express to them that one day someone else may need their help, and they will feel a bit of peace for their own act of giving.

In this you greatly rejoice, though now for a little while you may have had to suffer grief in all kinds of trials. These have come so that your faith—of greater worth than gold, which perishes even though refined by fire—may be proved genuine and may result in praise, glory and honor when Jesus Christ is revealed.

1 Peter 1:6–7

4

HANDMADE

I am convinced that God makes no mistakes when he puts people together. We are introduced to each other in various ways, perhaps through our workplace, our schools, our neighborhood, or our church. Then it's up to us to choose those who become our friends.

There is something special that I find very attractive about every friend of mine. For some it's the way they are sweet to their children. For others it's the respect I have for the way they treat their husband. For certain friends it's a talent they possess, such as how they decorate their home, how they keep their house clean, or even how organized they are with their grocery list. But I have to say that what attracts me the most is the way many of my friends work with their hands. Embroidering, sewing, beading, stamping, doing needlepoint, baking, forming clay sculptures, or oil painting—I could go on and on. I know someone who can do each of these things very well. I even have a friend who can paint with her teeth!

Most of these people can purchase a painting, buy a needle-point work that is already crafted, or in some cases, buy anything their heart desires. The fun and the challenge for them, though, lies in making the craft themselves. It takes fortitude, patience, and desire. And to me, that's attractive!

Kris is a friend of mine who served on the PTA board at our daughter's special school in Dana Point, California. She is married to an orthopedic surgeon, and she could have anything that money could buy. But she also has what I have, a child who would capture your heart. Money can't buy that.

Kris has a way of making anything she touches turn to gold. She makes her own clothing and sews her own draperies to cover the windows of the real-life castle she lives in. Every gift she gives to others has much thought behind it, and in most cases the gift is handcrafted by her. She finds pleasure in the things that really count.

While Tayler was in the second month of her hospital stay, Kris left a box on our doorstep that I found on my return home one day. I couldn't wait to open it. She had woven tiny pastel ribbons together with teeny pearl beads on invisible thread. All of this was to form a beautiful little hairpiece for Tayler's hair.

Kris had firsthand knowledge of how important it was for our babies to look sweet and beautiful amongst the tubing, machines, and sterility of the hospital trappings. She knew that I would appreciate a handmade gift. She takes pride in her work and knows how much I admire her for that.

It's a very kind gesture to send a purchased gift to a friend who is hurting, and it's always appreciated. But when you take

THOUGHTFUL SUGGESTIONS

1. If you are able to sew on a button or even tie a knot, you will be able to learn how to needlepoint. You can make your friend a Christmas stocking. Show her your unfinished work when you feel she is in need of a real pick-me-up. Let her know that you think of her with every stitch you sew, then present it again when you are finished.

2. Sew a friend a pillowcase or make him a pillow. How many times have you cuddled up to one whether you're just resting, rocking, reading a book, or letting it prop up your head while watching a good movie? Your friend will always think of you when he puts your pillow to use or just sees it grace a quiet spot in his home.

3. Paint someone a picture. It is such an amazing talent to be able to paint, draw, or sketch. My friend Joni says that the talent is in your mind. She was a talented artist before she became a quadriplegic from a diving accident. She hasn't relinquished any of her many talents, even when challenged by her restrictions.

4. Can you make a quilt? Do you have rubber stamps to make a greeting card? Maybe you can make a jar of apricot preserves and let your friend know that it was a pleasure to prepare a homemade gift just for her.

the time to gather materials you've chosen and make a special project for a friend, your dedication really shines through. You may not find it hanging on her wall, sitting on her couch, or decorating her hair. The gift will be worn on her heart. This special gift says that you cared enough to make the very best that you could for her. There is a lot of creating to be done. Be ready for your handmade works to come in handy for friends who are hurting.

For you created my inmost being;
  you knit me together in my mother's womb.
I praise you because I am fearfully and wonderfully made;
  your works are wonderful,
  I know that full well.
My frame was not hidden from you
  when I was made in the secret place.
When I was woven together in the depths of the earth,
  your eyes saw my unformed body.
All the days ordained for me
  were written in your book
  before one of them came to be.

Psalm 139:13–16

5

ALL GOD'S CHILDREN

We were fortunate that our first baby was Kara. When she had a doctor visit scheduled, it was just the two of us. On appointment days I could take the time to match her outfit to her blanket, match her hanging toy to her outfit, even match her pacifier to everything else. And if that weren't nauseating enough, I would match my outfit to hers also. Not to say that we had the greatest wardrobe. It was either pastels or primary colors—that was it! I had the time to organize it all, and I had the patience to keep it all together. Not so with baby number two. We had almost nothing together. Kara would be lucky if her shoes matched each other when I would send her off to school, much less matching her outfit.

While Tayler was a resident of Children's Hospital, there were many days and nights when I needed some help with Kara's care so that I could spend time with Tayler. Her teacher,

her teacher's aides, and many others came to my rescue. One friend put it this way: "Please let me take care of your girls when you need me. After all, they are really God's children, on loan to us anyway." She said this with a smile. I always offered money or at least offered to care for their children and return the favor when time permitted me to extend my help to them.

Brad and I had such a hard time dating each other after our children were born. It was financially impossible to go away for a weekend, and it was hard for us to leave the girls with others because each one's care was more than a handful.

One weekend we got creative with the help of Brad's parents and the generosity of United Cerebral Palsy (UCP) of Orange County. The UCP has a program that sends parents of a child with disabilities away for a weekend stay at various participating hotels. The stay was completely free for us. It was sent from heaven. The weekend without our girls gave us a reminder that we were still a couple too.

We were incredibly fortunate that we were able to entrust our children to Brad's parents during that time. It's always a stress reducer for parents to know that their child is being well cared for in their absence.

It makes sense that God would lend his children to us rather than let them go out altogether on their own. They are, however, a tremendous responsibility. Caring for a child is a challenge never to be taken lightly. When you are offering to care for your friend's child, know that it's not always easy for parents to let go of their young son or daughter. Treat these children as if they were your own while they are in your care. And always know that they are all God's children.

THOUGHTFUL SUGGESTIONS

1. Call a friend who is going through a hard time and offer to sit with her children. Pack a lunch and take them to a local park. Bring sand toys if the children are of the appropriate age.
2. If the children are older, take them to a suitable movie or to a musical play. Lunch afterward isn't a bad idea here either.
3. Take the kids to a library, museum, or amusement park. Treat them to a visit to the mountains, a lake, or the beach.
4. The little ladies might like to go out for a sip of tea and a bite of finger sandwiches. The little lads would love to break open a bag of salty peanuts and gulp down a Coke at a baseball game.
5. If it works for you to have them stay at your home and maybe even spend the night, it would no doubt relieve some tension caused by their family's stressful situation. Renting a movie with plenty of popcorn and lemonade is always a big hit. Morning pancakes or their favorite cereal is a simple breakfast. For a special treat at bath time, throw a towel into the dryer while they are bathing. A warm towel after a bath or shower will make them feel cozy all over.

For as high as the heavens are above the earth,
    so great is his love for those who fear him;
as far as the east is from the west,
    so far has he removed our transgressions from us.
As a father has compassion on his children,
    so the LORD has compassion on those who fear him;
for he knows how we are formed,
    he remembers that we are dust.

Psalm 103:11–14

6

"I CARE" PACKAGE

Tayler was just days old with two operations behind her already when we were told that she faced an incredibly long hospital stay if she were to survive her medical anomalies. It was to be another extended non-vacation getaway at our home away from home, the hospital. Undoubtedly, our friends were just as dumbfounded as we were to find out we'd be going through the same "General Hospital" routine again.

The days ran into each other. We stared at the monitors, just waiting until Tayler was stable enough to be held in our arms. Boredom reared its ugly head. The headaches were frequent due to the amount of tears that were shed, and I never had enough aspirin or supplies with me.

A great friend had been by to visit Tayler in the ICU several times, and each time she came, I wasn't there. She would leave sweet little notes at the crib to let me know she had been there.

She didn't live near the hospital, so I was especially touched that she would come so far and even more disappointed that we missed each other every time.

One day she came by and left us a package. It was more of a large gift bag, heavy with many items. All of the items were

THOUGHTFUL SUGGESTIONS

1. Take a similar package to your friends even if they are not in the hospital. You can tailor your package to address whatever circumstances they are going through. Enclose a card that expresses your concern for them. Let them know that there is more where that came from.

2. Wrap up things to open each hour of the day. Be clever. Maybe it's a granola bar and orange juice for the first hour, a journal for the next, a rented movie and popcorn for another surprise package. The hospitals have VCRs and monitors to use in the rooms. You get the picture.

3. Items should be inexpensive so that you can give your friend the practical things without spending a fortune. A pack of gum, breath mints, mouthwash, toothpaste, and toothbrush would be appropriate. (Make sure that these are not the only items included in the care package; your friend may think that you are sending her a not-so-subtle message.) Pick a wildflower or two to top off the gift.

4. For the adventurous person who is trying to heal, put together a "Mission Impossible" package. Of course the words written across this package will be, "This is your mission, should you choose to accept it." (Or make a creative cassette-taped message.) This box may include items like cheap sunglasses, a fake mustache, or a toupee. Give him a clue book that leads him to call you at a certain time. Then tell him that you are taking him to lunch or dinner, bringing food in, or whatever your detective mind can come up with.

useful and practical for a hospital stay. She didn't miss a beat. There were magazines, aspirin, candy bars (my favorite), fruit, warm socks, tissues, fingernail files, nail polish, and many other items that escape my immediate recall. It was enough to carry me through that week and more.

No matter what circumstances your hurting friends or loved ones are experiencing, there is never a time that they won't appreciate some small gift of thoughtfulness from you that shows that you care. When you put together your own "I Care" package to deliver to them, it will be a gift they won't forget.

> The LORD is close to the brokenhearted
> and saves those who are crushed in spirit.
>
> Psalm 34:18

7

MUSIC TO THEIR EARS

We have been attending our church for over fourteen years now, and we have seen a lot of changes and have played a tiny part in some of those as well. When Kara was six years old, I asked the children's ministry team if they would create a classroom for children with disabilities. Their response was, "Sure, go right ahead." Well, that wasn't quite what I had in mind. I couldn't head up the program with what was on my plate at home; I needed the benefits that the program would bring to our family. I needed a chance to go to church myself, knowing that Kara and our other two girls were appropriately cared for.

However, I did my research and found a woman who was willing to take charge and move in the direction that I had designed. She was terrific. Within a year or so, the baton was passed to another woman who ran the ministry for years until she had to move on also. That's when the church asked me to take over the administration of the ministry. At this time my little family was at a more stable place, and I felt that I might be able to take on the responsibility. I had been somewhat frustrated that not everything I wished for in the ministry was evolving, so I was excited to take on the challenge.

God put many people in place to help me create and run the programs I had longed to see in the ministry. One of these programs was a choir. I named them the Super Stars. It was a full-inclusion choir, which means that it was made up of both kids with disabilities and kids without disabilities. It was such a healthy combination, and we had a blast performing. Robin, a very talented musician and singer and mother of a daughter with cerebral palsy, was the choir director, and she was a trueborn motivator for these kids.

The most memorable performance was at Christmastime in 1999. We took several of the children and their parents caravanning to homes in nearby neighborhoods to sing Christmas carols. I can only imagine how the homeowners must remember these children with awkward gaits and wheelchairs and the healthy young children alongside them, assisting those who needed a little help to ring the Christmas bells or hold up the sheets of music.

The fondest memory of the evening was singing at the home of Linda and Bob Nelson. They had adopted eleven children, all with various disabilities. Linda brought out cookies and hot chocolate to the shivering carolers, who didn't mind the cold because of the heartfelt warmth of us all being together and seeing the smiles on the faces of our listening audiences. And if that were not enough, the evening was topped off with a message on my answering machine that

Thoughtful Suggestions

1. There is nothing more precious than the sweet sound of children's voices. Record your child or children on a cassette tape or CD and send it to various hurting people. Send a copy to the children's grandparents or great-grandparents. Their father will appreciate a recording too when he is traveling on business and missing his family. Tuck it into his suitcase before he goes on the road. Residents of convalescent homes drink up the voices of little children as well.
2. Find out who your hurting friend's favorite artists are. Purchase some of their tapes or CDs. No doubt this will bring a grateful smile to the face of your loved one.
3. Write a song of your own that expresses your compassion for what your friend is going through. Sing it a capella or put it to music that is already recorded. Sing it to the tune of a familiar nursery rhyme so he will recognize it and hum along.

was recorded during our stop at the Nelsons'. Someone had called my answering machine at just the right time to tape the children belting out one of the holiday hymns. It was just beautiful. I ran the message back over and over all season long. No one ever admitted to doing it, but it made my Christmas special just the same.

After many memorable performances, the Super Star choir disbanded. I will always cherish the times that we sang and played together under Robin's uniquely qualified direction. I will also treasure the recording made by the anonymous caller. It was a kind and thoughtful thing to do. It was more than music to my ears; it was a blessing, an unforgettable Christmas gift.

The LORD is my strength and my shield;
my heart trusts in him, and I am helped.
My heart leaps for joy
and I will give thanks to him in song.

Psalm 28:7

8

WHAT A CRACK-UP!

When Kara was born, she was not diagnosed immediately with anything, nothing too serious anyway. But after her emergency heart surgery at ten days old, things went swiftly downhill. The doctors were concerned about her recovery. Her healing was taking longer than they had anticipated, so they did a series of assessments on her. They did a brain scan, an audio test, and various cardio examinations. There were no definitive answers for weeks.

After her two-month stay, she was finally coming home. The night before her release, I asked the ICU chief physician to please level with me. I wanted to know what to expect for Kara's future. "How healthy or not healthy is our baby?" I asked.

The chief physician pulled up a chair and asked me to do the same. He proceeded to tell me that Kara's heart anomalies were so severe that she would not live past the age of five. Her hearing test indicated she would eventually be deaf, and her brain scan resulted in the prognosis of acute brain damage. He held my hand and quietly said, "She will live in a vegetative state all of her short life, and I highly suggest that you and your husband consider institutionalizing her."

I thought I was going to faint. My skin instantly turned cold and clammy. I was speechless. I just lowered my head in my hands when he walked away.

That evening I walked through the nearly empty parking lot and entered my room at the Ronald McDonald House. I cried. I sobbed, I wailed, and I asked God, "Why do you hate me so much?" Just as I said those words, I started to think of how God must be planning a miracle. I started to laugh and turn hopeful, almost giddy. I cried some more, and laughed, then I became anxious to call my faithful friends and ask them to pray with all of their might for this miracle. I also called our pastor. Then finally I called Brad. He would be driving down the next morning to escort his wife and baby home for Kara's first time. He had no idea what I had just heard from the doctor. He listened to my laughter, my tears, and my pleading, and he gave me no reply. But he agreed to pray with me over the phone. He would be waking up early the next morning to make the seventy-five-mile trip to the hospital and transport us home.

While I was trying to get some sleep, it suddenly dawned on me that in his mind Brad may have been searching out institutions where he could drop me off, then he would continue home alone with his new baby. He must have decided that I had gone out of my mind and was finally cracking up.

The morning came, and we swept Kara up, equipped with monitors and a discouraging diagnosis. We had a very quiet ride home. I figured that the miracle God was planning must need to be delayed.

Three months later, Kara had her first set of tubes placed in her ears to relieve the buildup of fluid behind both eardrums. Then when she turned six months old, her ophthalmologist informed us that Kara had hypoplasia of the optic nerve and that she would eventually be blind.

That did it. I had had just about enough bad news. I was tired—no, I was exhausted. I loved her and I never neglected her, but I felt strongly that it was time for me to jump ship. I decided to take my life. *If heaven is so great, then why can't I be there now?* I questioned myself. I didn't discuss my plans with anyone for fear they would try to talk me out of it.

My plans started out like this: On the first day of my suicide plot, I decided that the most convenient way to take my life would be to go to the garage, turn on the ignition of the car, and let the motor run until I fell asleep.

On the second day of my scheming, I started thinking about Kara. There would be no better person than her mother to care for her, so the only logical thing to do would be to carry her with me while she slept and hold her in my arms until we both fell asleep forever.

On the third and final day of my planning, I started to think of Brad. He is such a good guy, and it would destroy him to find his wife and baby this way. I would have to knock him out and drag him down with us. He weighed about 260 pounds and I was about 105 (give or take 5 pounds). Carrying him was not going to be easy. Another obstacle was that *we didn't have a garage!* I didn't know anyone that would lend me an enclosed car shelter for a mass suicide attempt (and I still don't).

THOUGHTFUL SUGGESTIONS

1. Make phone calls to friends or loved ones going through hard times. Don't assume that someone else is keeping them sane through the difficult situation they are facing.
2. Ask if you can come by to visit, and then ask how you might be able to give them respite from their daily routine if at all possible.
3. Ask how they are feeling about their spiritual faith during this awful time. They may have had a very strong faith in God before their hardship. And they may now need some affirmation from you that God still exists and still loves them.
4. Give them a daily journal to write their thoughts in—a place where they can safely jot down their emotions. It helps to write out our heavy hurts on paper.

To this day I have never revisited those brutal, suicidal thoughts. Thanks to support from my family and friends and their constant eagerness to cheer us, I now laugh at myself when I think of the foolish plans I had conjured up.

Do you know someone in a deep depression who could possibly have such feelings? Don't assume that he will be just fine with time. Be sure to have a listening ear and encourage him to open up so that he doesn't crack up.

He said to me, "My grace is sufficient for you, for my power is made perfect in weakness." Therefore I will boast all the more gladly about my weaknesses, so that Christ's power may rest on me. That is why, for Christ's sake, I delight in weaknesses, in insults, in hardships, in persecutions, in difficulties. For when I am weak, then I am strong.

2 Corinthians 12:9–10

9

PHONE HOME

y mother, my two brothers, and their families live
on the outskirts of Oklahoma City. My grandmother
and most of my extended family also live there. A couple of
years ago, my younger brother was going through a rough time
emotionally. He was having problems in his marriage and his
health was suffering. He and I are very close. There were times
that he would call me, and if I couldn't talk he would be greatly
discouraged. With such a long distance between us, talking on
the phone was all the communication that we had.

He was getting more and more despondent, so I began to
drop everything to speak with him whenever he would call.
Or I would be certain to pick up the phone and call him on a
daily basis. Michael is seven years younger than I am, but our
personalities are very similar—we could have been twins.

One evening in January he called and left an urgent message

that he needed to come out to California to see me. He said that he had something very important to tell me. I was a nervous wreck. He didn't give me any hints, and part of me didn't want him to, but in the absence of concrete facts, I drew my own unappealing conclusions:

1. He has a deadly virus.
2. He's interested in men.
3. He killed someone, and he wants me to hide him.

I saw some friends of mine the night before his arrival, and I asked them to pray that I would react well to his news, whatever it might be.

I picked Michael up at the John Wayne Airport in Orange County, and we drove down the coast to an exclusive restaurant that overlooked the ocean. The sound of the crashing waves could drown out our conversation if he didn't want anyone else in the world to hear him. With tears in his eyes, he said that he and his wife were getting a divorce. Honestly, I had no idea that their marriage would come to an end.

With a heavy two-hour talk behind us, I suggested that Michael and I go see a lighthearted movie. We were coming out of the theater arm in arm when the friends whom I had just asked for prayer the night before were coming right toward us.

It was Brad Budde and his beautiful wife, Nicki. He played football with my husband Brad at USC and then played professional ball for many years afterward. He is still a huge man. He and Nicki stood in shock at the sight of the two of us. They had forgotten our conversation the night before about my brother coming in from Oklahoma. I thought that Brad was going to pulverize Michael for linking arms with his friend's wife. Nicki said that her thoughts

Thoughtful Suggestions

1. Be sure to keep the phone lines of communication open with the ones you love, especially if they live a long distance from you.
2. Make a pact that you will call on certain days and at certain times. Check with your phone service for the hours when you can call at a discount.
3. E-mail is a great way to keep in touch, and it's free. It doesn't meet the need to hear a human voice, though.
4. I am the worst at calling my mother, brothers, grandmother, and others I love. I hope they know that I love them even though I don't call. I hope they still love me. But that's not something family members should have to assume. Please don't do as I do, but do as I say. Does that sound familiar?

were, "The old girl still has it in her to date a young, great-looking guy." Then I introduced the three of them to each other. It was hilarious. And in the end no one was killed, no one had a deadly virus, and Michael was still interested in women.

The sadness still exists, though, because of the split between two wonderful people, and because three beautiful girls are torn between their parents. Their lives should be full and rich again, given time. But the lines of communication are the key. Michael needed me to be there for him during his extremely difficult time. No matter where you are, be sure to phone home to those you love every chance that you get.

> A word aptly spoken
> is like apples of gold in settings of silver.
>
> Proverbs 25:11

10

GREAT DAY IN THE MORNING

Have you made some form of exercise an important part of your day? I'm a firm believer that exercise is not only a necessary evil for the body, but it is also important for the mind. Of course anything in excess is not good for us either. But getting into the habit of a simple daily routine is a good thing. If you know someone who is in a deep depression, invite her to be your exercise partner. It may be walking around the block three or four times or exercising to a videotape in your living room or garage.

I have always had a hard time fitting workouts into my daily schedule, so when it came time to lose thirty pounds (ugh!) I found the time to make it fit in. Believe it or not, my exercise ritual is five or six days per week at 4:30 in the morning. Being one who could sleep the day away, I can't believe it myself. I know that if I didn't have someone to be accountable to, I wouldn't let my toes touch the floor before 9:00 a.m. Thanks to my exercise buddies, and others, I am held accountable, and it works.

THOUGHTFUL SUGGESTIONS

1. Don't be overenthusiastic when suggesting an exercise idea to your friend. Let her know that you are in need yourself and that you would like a willing participant to partner with so that you can reach a healthful goal of your own.
2. If your friend who is going through a tough time is unable to leave his home because of a medical condition, present him with the idea of asking the doctor or therapist how you can help with exercise. It could be just bending a knee up and down or stretching feet and hands for him.
3. Go to her house in your workout togs, dumbbells and videotape in tow. If she doesn't mind, you can work out together there. Any exercise program can be altered to fit each individual's needs.

My exercise routine is also my social hour in my crazy life right now. I am working full-time as an office manager for a landscape architectural firm. I work the day shift while Brad is home with the girls until I return. Then he is off to work the night shift at the police department. All of our girls have a busy schedule after school, and once they are off to bed, I write. There really isn't any other time that I can exercise except in the early morning hours. I have learned to love walking under the stars and analyzing the moon in the darkness of the early day. It gives me the perspective I need to recognize the excellence of God and his creations versus the smallness of my sufferings. It also makes me feel like I have God's attention, and while I'm watching the dawn awaken, I know that it's going to be a great day!

Come near to God and he will come near to you.

James 4:8

11

FRUIT OF THE WOMB

In May 1999 I spoke about my girls to the congregation of Saddleback Community Church in Lake Forest, California. A phrase I used in my talk had to be altered at that time. Generally when I would tell about my pregnancy with Paige and the fact that we never had a medically positive experience, I would mention that we felt unfit to bear healthy children. I would say, "We weren't planning on having a third child; in fact we were using everything man had made to prevent another pregnancy, but Brad threw his boxers on the bed again and I got pregnant." Our pastor felt that a better way of saying that was simply to state, "Things happen, and I got pregnant." It's become somewhat of an inside joke. But I have to admit that I have used my old version since then. It seems to break the tension after my listeners have heard such a sad story about our other two girls.

Obviously pregnancy came easily to Brad and me, but not to some of our friends. Infertility is not something to be taken lightly. I have a close girlfriend who was unable to bear children, and she suffered with that painful reality for years. It was the cause of great heartache for her husband also. She underwent many operations to try to correct her inability to become pregnant. She asked her husband, her mother, and me to join her each time before she would enter the operating room. We would pray together and hold her hand all the way down the hallway to the wide swinging double doors. Then we would let

THOUGHTFUL SUGGESTIONS

1. Be what your friend needs. If she asks you to tell her, "Everything is going to be all right," then say it. Although you have no idea what will happen in the immediate situation, you must know that in the long run, it *will* be all right. Trust God to help you have the strength you will need to help her through this difficult time.
2. Don't try to say all the right words. If you have had even one child of your own, she won't believe you when you say, "I know how you feel." Frankly, you don't. Just stand by her side and be what she needs you to be, a loving, nonjudgmental, caring friend or loved one.
3. I have heard that some women keep their new pregnancies a secret from a friend who is unable to become pregnant. Even though you are trying not to hurt her with your good news, please share your enthusiasm gingerly. It will bring you closer. Most women I've heard from say that they would rather share in the joy of a friend's pregnancies than be left out. It may hurt, but there is even more hurt when they are excluded from their friend's or loved one's exciting news.

her know how much we loved her. We knew that she felt our support, and we knew how much she appreciated it.

It is very difficult to be unable to expand your family when you want to. Be sensitive and caring. Don't brag about your child's accomplishments to your friend who is hurting because of infertility. Her time has not yet come to boast of her children's endeavors, and maybe it never will. Let her see the qualities she admires about your family for herself. Encourage your children to refer to your friend as Auntie (if that is acceptable to your friend). This can bring a hint of healing to her and encourage a genuine fondness between you as friends.

> Everyone born of God overcomes the world. This is the victory that has overcome the world, even our faith.
>
> 1 John 5:4

12

HOW SUITE IT IS

In Kara's nineteen years, she has had twenty-three surgeries and procedures. She has won the medal of valor in our family for pure endurance and perseverance through the pain and inconvenience of recovery. She is our hero.

It was emotionally difficult for us to make it through the early years with Kara's diagnosis, her surgeries, hospital stays, and daily care at home. But it was completely physically feasible to do it all. When Tayler was born, it was extremely trying to handle being at the hospital for her and being everywhere else for Kara. Then when Paige was born, it threw a whole new dynamic into the mix, and it was impossible for me to be in three places at one time.

In September 1994 Kara was diagnosed with a urinary tract infection that landed her in the hospital. There was a miscommunication at the doctor's front office, and I eventually just took matters into my own hands and rushed her to the emergency room. She was in trouble. She was immediately admitted and tested for everything. With her heart history, the admitting doctor wanted to leave no stone unturned. Her symptoms were a high fever, no appetite, no energy when she *was* awake, and dehydration. After the third day of her hospital stay, they finally ruled out everything but a urinary tract infection.

All the while, Tayler was in the first grade and Paige was in kindergarten. Brad's work schedule could not accommodate this untimely hospital stay. That's when another great friend came into the picture.

Teri had three children of her own. She and I were high school song leaders together, and our husbands worked at the Newport Beach Police Department. Joe and Teri had two girls that are the ages of Tayler and Paige and a younger boy, Joey. Our two families blended together almost perfectly.

Teri knew about Kara's illness and was ready to jump in with everything she had to help out. She was another friend who would not take no for an answer, and she put on her thinking cap once more. She insisted upon coming to the hospital at 4:00 a.m. She said that she would just sleep in the chair beside Kara

---

THOUGHTFUL SUGGESTIONS

1. Can you find a way to relieve a caregiver for an hour or two? Make sure that your own family doesn't suffer because of your absence from them.
2. Call your hurting friend or caregiver and let him know when you have free time. Tell him that you don't know of anything else that you can do for him, but that you would love to give your time just to be there to help out.

until I returned or Kara awoke. This would relieve me each day so that I could go home and ready the other girls for school and see them off. Teri was a lifesaver. She had her own family to care for, but somehow she handled that too.

Teri is one of those friends who knew how to fill a need before I even realized what the need was. She played major roles on the PTA board. She owns and runs an interior drapery business. She coached her daughter's synchronized swimming team and won a gold medal in the Masters Champion World Games in Munich, Germany. She is a devoted wife and mother. For her to help me out and consider Kara's hospital room as a hotel suite for the wee hours of her morning made her a blessing beyond measure. She is a true-to-life angel, a dear friend, and I love her for *everything* she is.

I can do everything through him who gives me strength.

Philippians 4:13

PART 2

YOU CARE,
BUT GOD CARES
EVEN MORE

13

BREAKING BREAD

My birthplace is Oklahoma City, Oklahoma. I was raised in Southern California. My dad's dream was to live on the Pacific coast. He thought he could quench his quest for peace if he could make his way to the western shoreline. I was four years old when we left my aunts, uncles, cousins, and grandparents, whom we loved dearly. It was an exciting adventure for all of us though, even for me at such a young age.

We continued to have a sense of extended family because we would visit my dad's folks and cousins every summer for a reunion. We would taste that southern style cooking at my grandmother's house—chocolate cream pies and fried okra. My favorite was the pie. If my memory serves me right, at times when we visited, there would be a friend of the family who was in need. My grandmother would rally her girls together to make a meal for the hurting individuals, including her delicious pie, and go to the aid of her friends.

I was young then, so I assumed the distressed family didn't know how to cook and that some of Grandmommy's homestyle cooking would make them happy. I didn't realize they had circumstances outside of needing meals that made their situation so discouraging.

My mother and my brothers moved back to Oklahoma after my father died in 1980. It was a comfort to my mom to be near her grass roots and close to my father's grave. Brad was a native Californian, so moving to Oklahoma was not going to be an option for us.

Just before Tayler was born, my mom flew out to stay at our home for a couple of weeks. She realized she would be helpful to me with Kara once the new baby arrived. Since Kara adores my mother, it was a win-win situation. And it made coming home from the hospital with a newborn much easier to envision. We had no idea how valuable my mom would be to us.

Tayler was just three days old when she had her first emergency surgery. My mom stayed at home and cared for Kara, did the laundry, cleaned our town house, and made every meal for us. She was amazing. She had been living on her own, so she was accustomed to only taking care of herself. All of a sudden she was caring for four.

Before long, meals from friends started arriving after the news trickled out about Tayler's birth and her completely unexpected hospital stay. One after another meals came, until the freezer and refrigerator were almost full. Finally, my mom had a chance to let up a little and actually feel the impact of what had happened to her daughter, her son-in-law, and her new grandbaby.

I could never name each friend who took the time to help my
mother or help us through the hurting years with the luxury of

Thoughtful Suggestions

1. Ask the distressed family what their diet restrictions are. Ask
   how many people are staying with them in their home. Be sure to
   find out all you can so that the recipients will be able to benefit
   from your efforts.
2. When planning a meal for a troubled family, keep your own
   budget in mind. Don't be unnecessarily elaborate or gourmet if it
   will be a burden on your own family.
3. The biggest challenge of making a meal for a friend is balancing
   the time that is taken away from your own family just to do the
   preparation alone. Double the recipe when possible and prepare
   enough food for both your friend and for your family as well.
4. Make main dishes for your friend to keep in the freezer to
   pull out as needed. That's extremely helpful. Separate the meal
   into small, individually sized dishes. When going through a
   painful situation, not everyone is always hungry at the same
   time.
5. When possible, include the recipe with each dish. You have
   given them a gift that they may want to duplicate and distribute
   to someone else when time permits them to be able to reach out
   to others.
6. Use disposable containers whenever possible, but if you can't,
   make sure to label each container that you would like returned to
   you. Include your name and your phone number. Let them know
   that you will be by to pick up the containers yourself when they
   are done with them. Remind them that your phone number is
   on the container, and that they can call you again for any future
   help.
7. There are other chapters in this book that pertain to the giving
   of a meal. Please read on.

homemade meals. The cost of eating out for the six months of Tayler's hospital stay would have been overwhelming. Oh, we could have found a way to make it work, and we were prepared to face up to this challenge. But such a load is lifted when you know there is a meal prepared for you and you don't have to pay for it or exert one more ounce of energy to plan it!

Whenever possible, take your children with you to deliver your warm package when you help someone out with a meal. They will benefit from seeing what mom or dad, grandma or granddad, were doing with their time in the kitchen besides making a meal for their own family. Let your kids know the circumstances behind the friend's need for a home-cooked meal. They will grow up realizing (and hopefully imitating) several things about you as their parent or loved one: You are compassionate, you are giving, and you step up to the plate when there is a need to comfort a friend.

> Remember the days of old;
>   consider the generations long past.
> Ask your father and he will tell you,
>   your elders, and they will explain to you.
>
> Deuteronomy 32:7

14

KEEP THOSE CARDS
AND LETTERS COMING

Kara was born in Mission Viejo, California. Her first emergency operation was at San Diego Children's Hospital, which was seventy miles south of our home. It was difficult for our friends and family members to visit. Kara's initial stay in the ICU was two months long. I settled in at the Ronald McDonald House at the end of the hospital's parking structure, which gave me a temporary address.

After the first two weeks of Kara's stay, Brad went back to work near our home and enrolled in a master's program paid for by his employer. He also took on a self-motivating weight loss program and lost seventy pounds.

During that period of our lives, I functioned much like a robot at times. I found myself becoming somewhat of a martyr. My friends would offer to visit, and many did make the long trip to see Kara and me. But there were dry spells when I would ask them not to make the drive or put themselves out. Our friends wanted to be supportive, and I know that it was painful for them to watch us struggle through a difficult time. Even though I asked them not to travel out of their way, I did let them know

THOUGHTFUL SUGGESTIONS

1. If you are on a low budget, send a postcard to your friend who is hurting. The postage is slightly lower and the cards are generally less expensive than stationery or a greeting card.
2. In this computer age, send an e-mail. There is no cost to you. Many times there are inspirational poems, stories, or sayings that you have received from others, and you can forward them on to your friend. Make sure you know what her emotional state is before you send anything too serious or send something that may make light of her current situation.
3. Keep your supplies handy for a quick note to slip into the post box. When you're out running errands, don't forget to stock up on stamps. You don't want to write a note that is outdated by the time you get around to buying postage. ATM machines and even grocery stores are selling stamps now.
4. The most inspirational book in the world is the Bible. Include a comforting passage in your letter. Look in a concordance for a word that has come to mind about their situation; it will lead you to just the right Bible verse. It will take some research, but your friend is worth your time.
5. Card designer companies have made a greeting for every holiday. There is a card for Grandparents' Day, Secretary's Day, Halloween, and even Labor Day. Keep a card handy that you can pull out when you know someone who would be grateful to receive it.

that I had a mailbox at the Ronald McDonald House where I could receive mail.

So the cards and letters started coming in. Each day I would look forward to visiting the House's office to see if I had mail. I could read it when I wanted to. I could show true emotion without worrying about my makeup smearing. It was my contact with the outside world without having to speak at all. Words were hard for me to come by at that time.

Writing a note or sending a card was also an outlet for my friends. They could think about what they would say in advance so it would come out the way they wanted it to. Then when I wasn't too stressed out, I could write back. And when I did, it was like writing a journal of my feelings. It was a comfort just short of a physical hug.

When we can't prove the fault of anyone here on earth for a tragic or discouraging situation, we tend to place the blame on our Maker. It's natural to want to place blame. "How could God allow this to happen?" some say. When your friend is ready to share his feelings with you, don't encourage him to find fault in anything or anyone. Give him time to adjust to what has happened and to sort through his feelings.

Don't worry that you can't fix things. "Time heals all wounds." That statement is true, but please don't write that cliché in a letter. Just be a friend and send a note that simply says, "I'm thinking of you today, and I love you." State in your note that you will be available for her whenever she needs a shoulder to lean on.

> The LORD himself goes before you and will be with you; he will never leave you nor forsake you. Do not be afraid; do not be discouraged.
>
> Deuteronomy 31:8

15

DID YOU HAVE
YOUR WHEATIES?

Our girls have introduced us to some of the most giving people in the world. Among them is a woman named Judy. She is the mother of Tayler's third-grade school friend Rachel. My girls' elementary years were such fun days for me. I was the room mother for Tayler's third-grade classroom, and Judy was a big help.

I believe that part of what sparked the girls' friendship was that they both had two siblings, all sisters, and they both had a sister with a developmental disability. This was such a unique situation. They were bubbly, sweet, and friendly to each other.

Naturally, Judy and I would chat and make plans for our girls' social lives. One day she dropped by my house just to say hello. I was having one of those PMS mornings, and I didn't have many positive things to say about my day. I was embarrassed that I didn't have anything to offer Judy as a treat with coffee. We were not in a financial bind, I believe that my house was fairly clean, and I don't remember my socks having holes in them.

Judy was thoughtful, and I could tell that she just loved to do things for others. The following morning she left a shopping bag at my doorstep. It was filled with breakfast groceries. I recall thinking that I may have been acting as if I hadn't eaten anything in days. But I would have probably been a much better impromptu hostess if I had eaten my Wheaties.

I have a great friend who bakes chocolate chip banana bread for her neighbors and friends. I believe she has blessed so many people with her breads that she could make the loaves blind-

THOUGHTFUL SUGGESTIONS

1. Have you ever known people who simply cannot function before they've had the "Most Important Meal of the Day"? The older generation will remember the milkman, the guy who brought glass bottles of milk to your doorstep on request. Why not play milk-and-cereal man for a friend who could use a little shot in the arm in the morning? Make sure he is not on vacation before you leave groceries that could spoil if not eaten or refrigerated right away. In fact, call to make sure he's home. Let him know that he should check his doorstep as soon as you pull away. (Cell phones are great for that.)
2. Milk and cereal are not the only breakfast foods that can start someone's day out on the right foot. Have you ever thought of throwing another stack of pancakes on the griddle on a Saturday morning? Warm up the syrup, soften the butter, pack on the blueberries, and make another person's day.

folded. Isn't that a great legacy to leave to your children and your family? A gesture of giving done so often that it becomes second nature to you. What a wonderful lesson to learn.

> It was he [Christ] who gave some to be apostles, some to be prophets, some to be evangelists, and some to be pastors and teachers, to prepare God's people for works of service, so that the body of Christ may be built up until we all reach unity in the faith and in the knowledge of the Son of God and become mature, attaining to the whole measure of the fullness of Christ.
>
> Ephesians 4:11–13

16

FROM A DISTANCE

The girls were two, three, and seven when Brad started to work the night shift from 3:00 p.m. to 3:00 a.m., Monday through Friday, at the police department. The four of us ladies were home to fend for ourselves during the evenings, and sometimes we just got bored.

It took a lot of energy to get my girls prepared for the day and ready for an outing, so careful planning went into most of our jaunts on the town. Of course there was the neighborhood park that we would frequent, but sometimes we needed a night out without sand between our toes and teeth, or bruises from bumping into the playground equipment.

Everywhere we went people would stare at us, sometimes with a smile, sometimes with a question mark written all over their faces. They just didn't know how to ask the questions that came to mind. Children were the easiest to talk to because they were not as shy. They would ask about Kara, "Why is she in that chair? Can't she walk? Why doesn't she talk? What's her name? How old is she?" They were all so curious. Kara loved the attention, but only when there was a smile behind the questions.

I didn't venture out unless I felt ready to face the public who would sometimes become our audience. I also avoided an outdoor escape if I was in a foul enough mood to reply to their questions, "It's none of your business." If I reacted like that, I would have made one more person uncomfortable with people who have disabilities. So I chose the positive route, and I decided to be geared up for those whose reactions to my daughter's presence might not be so kind or understanding.

THOUGHTFUL SUGGESTIONS

1. Look for someone in a grocery store who might need a kind gesture from a stranger. If you have the means, pay for the groceries in his cart.
2. Do you have a neighbor whom you have noticed struggling to balance taking care of things at home, working outside the home, and caring for her kids? She may seem to be keeping it all together, and maybe she is. But you can bet she would love to have someone notice all the things she does. You have her address. Just slip her a note that says that you appreciate her. Everyone needs encouragement, even those who seem to manage without a hitch.
3. Have you ever read a newspaper article that touched your heart so much that you wanted to say to the writer, "Good job" or "Keep it up" or "You touched my heart"? Go ahead and do it. Write a note to the editor of the newspaper and mention the article, subject, and the writer of the piece. Send it in to the newspaper office. The letter will be forwarded.

One night after we had saved our money, we planned to sup at a local restaurant. After we settled at our table, I noticed an elderly gentleman watching us from a distance. Every now and then I would look up and see his smiling eyes looking in our direction.

It took some time for me to finish a meal with my three little girls. Utensils dropping, water glasses spilling, bibs drooping. Spaghetti was never the meal to eat while dining in public!

Just as I was ready to gather up my messy clan, the waitress walked up to our table and said that an older man had paid for our dinner. I knew it had to be the gentleman from across the room, so I looked over his way and saw him walking briskly out of the restaurant. I couldn't even thank him, but I don't believe he needed my thanks.

Let people know that they are special, needed, or appreciated. The next time you are out naturally observing people, you might think to yourself, *I wonder what I could do to put a smile on the face of someone who seems to be hurting?* Maybe it's as simple as putting a smile on your own face.

> The LORD looks down from heaven
> on the sons of men
> to see if there are any who understand,
> any who seek God.
>
> Psalm 14:2

17

I'll Have a Grande, Non-Fat, Lo-Cal, Decaf Latte, Please!

Kara was thirteen when she joined her first baseball team. Within our city's district league there was a division called Challenger for children with disabilities. That's how we met Kelsey, her mom, Tane, and her dad, Doug. Brad and Doug looked like brothers, and they had an instant rapport on the field while they coached and assisted their girls. Tane and I became friends as the season progressed.

At a play day at one of our houses, Kara and Kelsey would have fun with Play-Doh, making cookies, reading books, and playing Chutes and Ladders, all with a little help from us moms.

Kelsey had been homeschooled for most of her little life. She had many medical anomalies that excluded her from being mainstreamed in a closed classroom setting with other children. A common virus or bacteria innocently transferred could prove fatal for Kelsey. We were very careful not to get together if any of my girls had the slightest cold.

In the summer of 1999, Tane finally decided to take a trip to Hawaii, where her mother, sister, and niece lived. She planned on taking a nurse with her to assist with Kelsey, bought her tickets, and was emotionally ready to go. Kelsey needed twenty-four-hour nursing care; her list of things requiring medical involvement was astounding. Just days before the trip, Kelsey was admitted to the ICU. There she stayed until just before Christmas. All the while, Tane spent the nights with her, sleeping in a recliner chair in Kelsey's isolated room. Doug was only able to visit on the weekends because of work. He was a film director in Los Angeles, and the hospital was in San Diego, where Kara had her heart surgeries.

After their return home, the three of them settled into the daily routine again of Kelsey's physical and occupational therapy, nursing shifts, doctor visits, and home tutoring. Tane and I chose one day a week that I would visit her in their home. I would stay for about an hour in the morning. We both loved coffee drinks, so we started to have fun with it. I would bring us both a different coffee beverage and a couple of scones just about every Tuesday morning.

We started out with simple lattes, and it went on from there. Sometimes I would surprise her with something we had never tried before. It was a special treat for a special time.

Of course, the morning hour isn't the only time to take your friends something special. Set a date and let them know that you just plan on visiting for a short while and it would be your pleasure to provide their favorite potion of the hour. Take a

THOUGHTFUL SUGGESTIONS

1. If your friend drinks coffee, hot chocolate, orange juice, or another favorite, make a date with her and provide a refreshing treat.
2. With the abundance of coffeehouses in most every town, it isn't hard or expensive to share a cup with a friend. Maybe you can meet at a café, or you can offer to swing by and share a ride.
3. After your morning walk around the lake or run through the woods, stop by the home of a neighbor you know could use a listening ear over a warm cup of tea.
4. If it becomes a routine with you and your friend, buy some cute matching cups that you two will use just for those special visits. Have a picture of the two of you imprinted on the outside. Or make a matching set of cups at a ceramic painting store.

card with you that they can read after you've left their home, a simple note that says, "I think about you when I can't be there to visit with you." They will look forward to your smiling face and your thoughtfulness when you bring them a cup of what "ales" them.

> The LORD longs to be gracious to you;
> he rises to show you compassion.
> For the LORD is a God of justice.
> Blessed are all who wait for him!
>
> Isaiah 30:18

18

PICTURE THIS!

How many times have you wished you had brought the camera for that once-in-a-lifetime shot? Too often we are too caught up in the moment ourselves to capture anything on film for that candid memory on glossy paper.

I have countless photos and videos in my possession that were taken by someone other than Brad or me. Now that I have the time to do more than put my nylons on in the car and brush my teeth using the steering wheel as the bathroom counter, I have been able to take more of my own pictures of my children. It's just a shame that the girls are almost old enough to use a darkroom themselves to actually develop the photos!

Tayler came home from the hospital in June 1989. Her birth month was January. The hospital's nursing staff and our girls' general surgeon gave Tayler a good-bye party. Brad and I brought Kara, thank-you gifts, goodies for the party and staff, and suitcases to carry all of Tayler's belongings home in. Two dear friends of ours knew what was going on with us that day, and they offered to videotape the party as well as the homecoming. They followed us from the hospital to the car and all the way home to Tayler's pastel bedroom, which had been awaiting her arrival

THOUGHTFUL SUGGESTIONS

1. Keep a camera loaded and handy at all times. When you are visiting your hurting friends or invited to a party in their honor, you'll have it ready to capture the memory of your time with them on film. Remember that they may not be in a photographic mood, but you can photograph something silly that their pet is doing, or maybe their children can muster up a goofy or smiley face.
2. Have your pictures promptly developed. There is something about receiving a note in the mail with a picture of a memory. Send it right away in a homemade frame, or just slip it inside a card that reads something like, "It was so great to visit with you on this day. I look forward to spending more time with you soon."
3. Michelle owns a home-based business that promotes memory books and memory album accessories for every occasion. She created an album that was specifically designed for Kelsey. It was priceless. Kelsey's own photos were framed on these pages. It gave her something special to look at while she had extended hospital stays. This gift for Kelsey and her parents is a cherished one, no doubt.
4. Teri gave me the idea to use photos as a party favor. She would have an appropriate backdrop made specially for the event and pose each child next to the birthday girl for an instant memory to take home that very day. (Of course, an instant camera is needed for this task.)

for months. We are so grateful to have that video. Thank you, Scott and Darla!

Kara underwent her first heart surgery at the time that Linda came to visit us in San Diego. Linda is a prolific picture taker and a doer for everyone else. She took numerous pictures of Kara while Brad or I held her. Kara was all bundled up in a receiving blanket and a knit cap to keep her temperature up. She was just three pounds when her first operation took place. Linda used the best of the pictures she had taken that day to make us a special gift. It is a Christmas ornament that hangs on our tree each year, nineteen years so far.

Is a picture worth a thousand words? It most definitely can be! While there is nothing like being there, some family members or friends don't always have the opportunity to be present. Having a picture to help express an experience takes the story to the next level.

Another way to make good use of photography is to keep a picture of your hurting friend on your refrigerator or your desk at work, or use it as a bookmark. It will remind you to pray for her and/or to find a way to cheer her up during a hard time in her life.

> Remember those earlier days after you had received the light, when you stood your ground in a great contest in the face of suffering.
>
> Hebrews 10:32

19

WHAT AN INSPIRATION!

Tayler was only three days old when she was admitted to the Children's Hospital and had immediate surgery. She had the first bed in the ICU when we walked through the double doors. To Tayler's right was a four-year-old boy. He had muscular dystrophy. He was incredibly patient and sweet. He was very familiar with the nurses and the hospital surroundings. His mother and I would talk when she could visit. I would fill her in with stories of the cute things he had said to the nurses and doctors. She would reply with a compliment of some kind for Tayler.

When we were unable to be at our children's bedside because of our other children's or husbands' needs, there were volunteers who would come and just sit with our young ones, rock them, hold them, feed them, or even sing to them. My good friend Margo was one of those sweet women who did all of the above for Tayler.

These volunteering women like Margo had experiences of their own that led them to care for another person in need. Knowing Margo and the challenges that she had faced and seeing her smile day after day, put one foot in front of the other, and just keep on going inspired me to do the same.

I believe that we have been placed on this earth to be examples of God's love for all of us. In everything we do, we should live our lives so that we can be an inspiration for others. You may not even have to say a word because your works and actions will speak volumes to those who are willing to watch and listen. When you are asked the question, "Would you tell me about yourself?" then the door is wide open and your story can unfold.

None of us will escape a hardship of some kind during our lifespan. But when the tough times come, there is someone who can relate to you and who has been through something similar. Hang on to the one who can keep a stiff upper lip and still give thanks to our Lord who gave us life in the first place.

THOUGHTFUL SUGGESTIONS

1. If you are at a place in your life where you have time to devote to others, maybe even helping people whom you've never met, check into local volunteer positions.
2. Apply to a hospital or care facility as a volunteer. Be sure to let the administration know what you are comfortable doing for a patient.
3. Find a ministry at your church that requires the expertise you can bring to it with your life skills.
4. Call a local shelter for the homeless. They will appreciate whatever help you can give them, whether serving food, cleaning the facility, or talking to the houseguests.

As for the mother of the boy who neighbored Tayler in the ICU, somehow she and I seemed to inspire one another. God truly gave the two of us only the situations that we could personally handle. One day she said to me, "I don't know how you do it." She continued, "I don't think that I could be a mother of a developmentally handicapped child." I replied that she inspired me with her own challenges. Her two sons both had muscular dystrophy. The boys, two and four years old, would not live into their teen years. My eyes fill with tears even now just wondering if they are alive today. I watched this mother work with her darling boys. She would push two tiny wheelchairs, both with oxygen tanks in tow. Even still, the smile on her face would cheer up a stranger. That's what I call an inspiration.

> Your attitude should be the same as that of Christ Jesus:
> Who, being in very nature God,
>> did not consider equality with God something to be
>> grasped,
> but made himself nothing,
>> taking the very nature of a servant,
>> being made in human likeness.
>
> Philippians 2:5–7

20

WE ALL SCREAM
FOR ICE CREAM

Do you ever feel like screaming? I mean really screaming! Your frustration level has hit new heights, and there is no way out as far as you can see. You know that today was a hard day, and tomorrow doesn't look too promising either. I have to say that I'm not proud of my screaming moments, and I have had more than my share. My undeserving little family has weathered more of my unhappy times than their fair share too.

I am writing about some of these instances not to brag about how defiant I can be or how unreasonable, impatient, or unloving I can sound. I tell you these stories because you just might have friends who have experienced similar meltdowns. Before they make one more person suffer through their screaming, they might just need to be taken out for a break, a time-out, or maybe a little ice cream. Try it—it could work.

It was another normal Monday. Brad was in the police academy, Kara depended on a feeding tube to survive, Tayler didn't know how to eat a full day's meal by mouth yet, and Paige was just three months old, with colic. It was a blistering 97-degree day in January—Southern California weather. We were hot, sweaty, and tired, and just about to end our lovely day of whining, feedings, vomiting, and continual crying. Oh, did I mention that Paige had colic? I wondered where the Colic Hospital was. It was enough to drive a mother insane. I finally forgave myself after months of self-help therapy for the act I'm about to describe.

Paige was crying in her swing while I had Tayler and Kara propped up for their evening feedings by way of gastrostomy tubes. It was easier and more time efficient to feed them simultaneously, so that's what I generally did. This night was no different than usual, except for the frustration level that I had reached.

Gravity pulled the liquid formula down a syringe that was connected to tubing surgically inserted into both Tayler and Kara's stomachs through the skin. In order for the fluid to descend, the girls needed to be relaxed and quiet. When they were agitated, their stomachs would constrict, which made it impossible for the food to flow down. When they would cry, time would stand still and I would be left holding two syringes while trying to calm two little girls and also one colicky baby in the swing behind me.

With all three crying at once, one night I just snapped. Before I did, though, I sang to them, shushed them quietly, told them bedtime stories, and recited Dr. Seuss books until I was turning blue in the face. I finally screamed, *"STOP CRYING!!!"* And

104

like a stubborn little child, I said out loud, "Okay, fine then, if you won't stop crying, then you won't be eating." And with that, I disconnected the tubing from both girls' syringes and hurled the cylinders full of liquid food across the dining room and against the wall. *Well,* I thought, *that will show them!* Oh, sure. Show whom? I had to clean up the mess! Just then my little Kara, who could barely crawl, creeped over to Tayler with all her might, lay down next to her, and rested her tiny arm across Tayler's even tinier chest as if to say, "I'll protect you from our Really Mean Mommy."

Another feeding-related incident would be enough to send anyone screaming. My girlfriend Sandy was looking for a swimsuit model for her new sportswear/swimwear catalog, and she

THOUGHTFUL SUGGESTIONS

1. Keep an eye on your friend with young children. Call and ask if she would like to take a stroll to the local soda shop or ice-cream counter. Sounds like I'm living in the '40s? These places really do still exist. You just don't sit at the counter anymore, you stand in line for hours, and then you take thirty minutes to decide what flavor you want after you've enraged the clerk by asking to taste each flavor in the freezer window.
2. Show up at your friend's doorstep with a half-gallon of his and your favorite ice cream. If you don't know what his favorite is, just guess. He will be delighted that you thought of him at all.
3. Remember that if people are diabetic, as much as they would like to, they can't indulge in the typical yummy stuff. If you don't know such information about your screaming friend, neighbor, or acquaintance, then show up with both diabetic ice cream and the real thing.

asked me if I would come with her to Los Angeles. I told her
that the only way I could go was if I brought Kara with us. She
desperately wanted a second opinion, so she said, "Let's do it."

Sandy had made several appointments for the day to interview
models at different agencies. By midday we had made it through
two or three agencies in Hollywood, and no one refused me
entrance with the baby and her stroller.

Then there was the most important, top modeling agency
in California, one of the top two in the nation. That was our
next and final stop. It was around noon, and I had fed Kara
before I entered the agency. Sandy had gone in before me
and was seated in the president's office, where I joined her.
The room had a panoramic view of the Pacific Ocean and
beautiful downtown L.A. All I remember is that there were
windows everywhere. The owner and president herself peeked
into the office to let us know that the models would be right
in, and then quickly she closed the door. Just then Kara pro-
jectile-vomited onto the glass table, the glass-topped desk,
and all over her stroller. I quickly turned the carriage around
so that the head of the stroller with the sun guard expanded
was facing the models as they came into the room. My hands
were dangled inside the stroller, and vomit was dripping off
my fingertips. But my poker face was giving my opinion as to
which models I felt had the look that Sandy was hoping for.
Sandy motioned them to turn around for a back shot, and then
they exited the room. We moved faster than we ever had in
all our lives. Grabbing every cloth or piece of clothing that
wasn't already soiled, we cleaned up the prestigious office,
and then I went with Kara down the hall and out of the ten-
story building. My apologetic heart was pounding; I couldn't
get out of there fast enough.

Sandy and I both decided that that day's occurrence was the most uncomfortable, sweaty, silently screamy moment we have ever experienced. And I don't remember where we went from there, or even how we got home. But I can safely say that we *didn't* stop for ice cream, although it wouldn't have been a bad idea.

> The eyes of the LORD are on the righteous
>   and his ears are attentive to their cry; . . .
> The righteous cry out, and the LORD hears them;
>   he delivers them from all their troubles.
>
> Psalm 34:15, 17

21

A ROSE GARDEN

We thought that we would never be able to buy a home with all of the financial debt that we had incurred. Although we were able to hang on to our condo by the skin of our teeth, we constantly prayed that eventually God would allow us the luxury of owning our very own single-family dwelling.

When God's timing was right, we gave our realtors a run for their money. We searched for months. It was difficult to find a home that fit with our need for a room on the ground level for Kara. She needed a bathroom of her own for her special equipment, and we wanted a bedroom for each of our other two girls. We were looking for all of this for the tiny little price that was within our budget.

Then one day, John and Rayetta stumbled across the house that would meet all of our needs. These two professional people made miracles happen, and we were able to buy a home that went above and beyond our expectations. It had five bedrooms, four bathrooms, a backyard a tad bit larger than a postage stamp, and a rose garden of our very own.

I never knew how much I loved roses until I watched them grow and bloom outside of my windows every day. Then I became fascinated with the different varieties and attracted to the perfumed flower.

A group of ladies who had prayed for a home for us for years came to give us a housewarming soon after we moved in. I will never forget my friend Evelyn, who brought me a vase of gorgeous flowers. There were seven beautiful roses that bloomed from only one stem; they came from her own beautiful garden.

Roses became a gift of love for me like no other. Brad sent a dozen roses to me at work one day out of the blue. They melted my heart. On my fortieth birthday my brothers sent me a gorgeous dozen. But the most touching and awesome bouquet of them all was the vase of forty different-colored, long-stemmed roses that were delivered to me by my mother. It was a breathtaking sight.

Remember that it's the giver who usually receives the most pleasure out of giving, so take pride in selecting the roses you choose to display or to give. There are many books and classes on how to prune and care for your beautiful flowers. What I love about rose bushes is that the more you prune them, the more blossoms will be produced. It seems like another natural gift from God. The more you give, the more you will receive.

And if we know that he hears us—whatever we ask—we know that we have what we asked of him.

1 John 5:15

Thoughtful Suggestions

1. Someone is always moving in or moving out of the neighborhood, and apprehension is usually present for the neighbor who is moving in. A vase or bouquet of flowers would be a sweet welcome gift for your new friend on the block. It shows that you are not a cranky neighbor and that you would be more than willing to loan that cup of sugar when needed.

2. Children love to bring a gift to their teacher on the first day of school. A wrapped rose with the thorns detached and a ribbon finishing the package is a great way to say, "I'm one of your new students, and I appreciate you as my teacher."

3. The garden is beautiful when it's full with roses, but so is your home on the inside. Display a vase of roses on the dining table set for dinner, like the Norman Rockwell portrait of the perfect family. The roses won't make the family perfect, but they sure smell and look good. (Don't forget to remove the tiny outside creatures that naturally crawl on the rose petals—there is almost nothing worse than a little green worm making its way through your lasagna.)

4. Roses are a wonderful way to say, "I'm sorry," "I love you," or "You are special to me, and it makes me sad to see you hurting."

5. If you have out-of-town guests staying with you, it's fun to pretend that you run a bed and breakfast. Have a tiny bud vase with a single rose on their nightstand. Then top it off with a mint on their pillow.

6. Don't wait to have company to grace the bedrooms with roses. All of my girls appreciate them too. Even Brad knows that I'm thinking of him when I fill a sort of masculine-looking vase (if there really is such a thing) with roses and place it on his nightstand. It's just a thoughtful thing to do, and it might ease a lingering sadness with its elegant beauty.

22

A Tisket, a Tasket

I had been publicly speaking to different audiences about the story of my girls' lives for about eight years before my own church asked me to tell it to the whole congregation. It meant that I was to stand in front of a total of fourteen thousand people over five different services. Talk about having butterflies!

The day after I spoke at our church, Brad and I had an opportunity to spend a week in Lake Tahoe. I sure needed the time to regroup. Brad was a vice detective at the police department then and he had a convention to attend there. We paid for my ticket, the girls were in good hands at home with childcare, and we were off. Brad spent much of the time in meetings, so I had plenty of free time to myself. That's where the thought of writing this book came to me. One afternoon it just hit me how blessed Brad and I had been to have such incredible people in our lives who made our situation a little easier to deal with. I sat for a couple of hours one morning and thought of each chapter heading. I haven't changed a single one.

That evening we went on a dinner cruise on the lake with the other police detectives and their wives. While searching for a seat at a table, I saw Linda, a friend of mine whom I had worked with years before. Linda's husband, Bill, was a detective on the Los Angeles police force. They were with other friends and they invited us to join them.

During our conversation I told them of my book idea and Linda's friend Jean told me about a wonderful idea of her own.

THOUGHTFUL SUGGESTIONS

1. For people with the cold or flu, gather appropriate items for a basket such as aspirin, cans of chicken noodle soup, a small box of Saltine crackers, a package of tissues, and a thermometer. A magazine that you know they would enjoy reading would be nice. Imagine the things that your mom would provide for you and throw those in too.
2. For the person who has just lost a loved one, put together a large basket of homemade food items: breakfast breads, fresh-squeezed orange juice, a breakfast quiche. Include enough for the out-of-town relatives who will be houseguests for the next few days.
3. For the person who has a long-term illness, ask if you can sit with her for a few hours and bring a basket of goodies with you, like Little Red Riding Hood. Rent a video that your friend would enjoy and put a couple of microwave popcorn packs in your basket. Include snack items that you know your hurting friend can have. Add a crossword puzzle, an everyday inspirational calendar, a couple of bottled waters, and some chewing gum or mints.

She said that she and a group of ladies from her church had made baskets of goodies for years to give to a person who is going through a hard time. She would wrap each basket with clear plastic wrap, and a ribbon completed the package. The contents of her baskets were unique and incredibly thoughtful. Such a gift could lift anyone's spirits.

The greatest thing about putting together a basket full of items to uplift a friend is the giver's spirit behind it. Jean's caring attitude and how she described the love behind each basket was what drew me to her in our short visit together in Lake Tahoe. She was so full of life that I could just imagine her humming the old familiar song while she put her gift packages together: "A tisket a tasket, a green and yellow basket . . ." Have fun with this great idea. You can bet that your hurting friend will have fun as the receiver too.

He who began a good work in you will carry it on to completion until the day of Christ Jesus.

Philippians 1:6

23

BRINGING IN THE HOLIDAYS

Frank was a neighbor of ours when we lived in our first little condo. His wife had a baby just one month before Kara was born. The two divorced while their daughter was a toddler. It just about broke Frank's heart. His ex-wife and their daughter moved north to live with her family. Frank left the military, in which he had served for several years, packed up his huge duffel bag, and we drove him to the airport. We had a sad feeling that we wouldn't be seeing Frank again.

He is a unique person. He would literally give the shirt off of his back to a stranger. We heard stories of how he gave a transient his last dollar, picked up hitchhikers everywhere he went, and did acts of kindness all over the world while he traveled in the military. He would light up a room when he walked in. I believe with all of my heart that Frank was behind some anonymous gifts that were given to us.

Frank kept in touch with us from Georgia, where he had finally landed. Surrounded by his family, he was in his element. Being there again he loved life and his folks, and he was embraced by family traditions.

He met his new bride-to-be on a bus during his travels across the country, and immediately he fell in love. Jan and Frank married, and shortly after their wedding he reenlisted in the Marines. They were relocated to Hawaii and eventually transferred to California. He was again based at his original location, which put them in a city close by our home.

Shortly after relocating to California, they had their first baby, Brianna. She was such a cute thing. The minute I saw her, just hours after she was born, I knew only a fraction of what they were about to face. Brianna was born with Down's syndrome. Jan was the best mother in the world for her sweet baby girl.

Early in her first year it was discovered that Brianna also had a form of leukemia that is somewhat common for children with Down's syndrome. The therapies and hospitalizations that they all endured were reported in the *Los Angeles Times*. The reporter of the *Times* befriended the family while she wrote a series of newspaper articles that followed the treatment and progress of this little angel. Brianna needed a bone marrow transplant to continue to live. A donor from New York was a perfect match, and so the operation process began.

It was the Christmas season, and it was very hard to spend the holidays in the hospital. We had experienced that too, so we wanted to spend our Christmas Day with them. I made the turkey dinner and all the fixings as if we were eating at home, and when the last dish was out of the oven we headed off for the hospital. Frank and Jan knew that we were on our way with lunch. Our girls were young and excited to be bringing

THOUGHTFUL SUGGESTIONS

1. Bring a holiday feast to friends who are hurting no matter where they are. It doesn't have to be made from scratch. Some grocery stores pre-cook dinners to be warmed up. Just call one to two weeks ahead to reserve a meal for your friends. Be sure to call your friends ahead also. Let them know that you will supply that holiday treat for them.

2. Christmas, Thanksgiving, and Easter don't have to be the only holidays that deserve a banquet. What about green oatmeal on St. Patrick's Day—remember *Green Eggs and Ham*? A little food coloring goes a long way. (Thanks for that idea, Carleen.)

3. Bake a heart-shaped cake or cookies on Valentine's Day. Ice the cake with pink, white, or red frosting. Decorate the cake with the words, "Be My Valentine." Everyone wants to be somebody's valentine on Valentine's Day.

4. Visit your friend on the Fourth of July covered in little American flags. Stick them in your pockets or tuck them in your belt. Wear them in your hair. Get patriotic. Your goal is to bring a smile to the face of your hurting friend.

5. It's Halloween, so wear a mask and bring a trick or a treat. If you have an extra mask for your friend, you two could be twice as silly.

6. The New Year is not always happy, so take your friend a bottle of what cheers him and a set of glasses to toast with, and make a resolution wish that the New Year will bring some hope into his current situation.

7. Get creative, get playful, or just be thoughtful. Know that illness, depression, and heartache have no gaiety, but when a national holiday goes uncelebrated because of difficulties, there is an even bigger sense of loss.

homemade takeout somewhere other than the park. We looked awkward, I'm sure, hauling a fully cooked turkey and trimmings up to the oncology wing of the children's hospital. But I'll never forget the look on Frank and Jan's faces when we rolled up with a completely cooked Christmas meal!

Brianna almost celebrated her second birthday here on earth, but God took her home before that day. The family, their friends, the doctors, and even the bone marrow donor did all that they could to bring healing to that adorable little girl.

We treasure the moments spent that Christmas with Frank, Jan, and Brianna. Memories like that never fade away. It was a true pleasure to give just a little bit of ourselves when we brought in the holiday for our friends.

May the God of peace, who through the blood of the eternal covenant brought back from the dead our Lord Jesus, that great Shepherd of the sheep, equip you with everything good for doing his will, and may he work in us what is pleasing to him, through Jesus Christ, to whom be glory for ever and ever.

Hebrews 13:20–21

PART 3

GROUP GIVING

24

I WANNA HOLD YOUR HAND

I t was the summer of '95, and my girls were stable and doing well. Brad was working a shift that allowed me some time for myself. I had three days per week when I would be able to devote some hours to reading, exercising, meeting with a friend, or just lying out in the sun. It was great to have that luxury.

Another good high school friend of mine, Kathy, was a cheerleader with me in our sophomore year. She was (and still is) incredibly beautiful and was every guy's heartthrob and the nicest girl in the world. Kathy fell in love with a boy from across town and stole his heart. Kirk attended our rival high school. He was gorgeous too. They were a picture-perfect couple. Their future was set. After they were married, he soon finished podiatry school and opened his own practice a year later. But soon after the practice was underway, Kirk was diagnosed with multiple sclerosis. This disease is uncommon for men to contract, and so it was difficult for doctors to speculate what his condition would eventually be. He was left without a true prognosis.

Kirk immediately had to be put on disability because he couldn't work with his hands. They were shaky, unstable, and at times just numb. His physical abilities grew worse in a short amount of time. Kathy worked hard at an aerospace corporation while nurse's aides cared for Kirk during the days and sometimes the nights.

Home health care agencies are sometimes hard-pressed to be able to fill a shift with a registered nurse. There were many days when nurses wouldn't show or call to say that they wouldn't be coming. Kirk and Kathy became painfully familiar with this unstable situation, and they tried to fill some of the shifts with help from friends and family members. Kirk was comfortable with me helping him with certain needs because he was completely aware of my situation with my girls and their medical conditions, and my father and his medical conditions also. I felt privileged to be one of those whom Kirk allowed to care for him.

There were many days that I would come to help and find many of his physical needs already taken care of. He would always greet me with a smile, and sometimes he simply wanted me to sit at his bedside, talk to him, and hold his hand.

Kirk loved his wife and son, Bradley, more than life itself. I believe that in the end it was his heartache, the thought of losing his family, and the hope of what might have been for them that enabled him to survive as long as he did.

The funeral ceremony that Kathy arranged for Kirk was touching but difficult; it was such a shame that he died at the young age of thirty-four. Many friends stood up and spoke of the memories they had of Kirk and of their commitment to sup-

Thoughtful Suggestions

1. Call ahead, ask if you can sit by your friend's or loved one's side and read him a book or bring over a video to view with him.
2. Bring lotions and a nail file. Give your friend a manicure or pedicure or both.
3. Give your friend a new hairdo. Or maybe a shampoo. Be aware that perfumes may be difficult for your friend to be around. Ask questions before you simply show up.
4. Take dictation for your friend. She may want to send a card or a letter to a loved one or an acquaintance, realizing that the world doesn't stop when her own is upside down. As long as we are still on this earth, we all want to know that we can encourage someone else in her time of trouble or need.

port Kathy and Bradley in Kirk's absence. I regret that I let my insecurities get the best of me, and I didn't allow myself to stand in front of our peers and share my very close experiences with Kirk and Kathy in the last year of his life. It was a blessing for me to be a part of this heart-rending situation as he ministered to me with his words of undying love for Kathy.

Kathy has seen a tragically harsh side of life, and she carried herself through it with refinement and complete dedication to her husband. I thank her for allowing me the chance to watch her grow and watch him die with dignity and finally rest in the arms of our Lord.

Several years passed before Kathy allowed herself to fall in love again. Just a couple of years ago, she married a wonderful man who proudly cares for Bradley as his own and provides the hope for a long future together.

I am grateful that I was allowed the time to be used by God when a friend needed my help. Just simply holding Kirk's hand brought peace to him. If you are given a window of opportunity to comfort someone, the memory of those short moments will last much longer than the moment itself.

> Even though I walk
>> through the valley of the shadow of death,
> I will fear no evil,
>> for you are with me;
> your rod and your staff,
>> they comfort me.

Psalm 23:4

25

GETTING FROM A TO B

Transportation is taken for granted when the car is not in the shop, when two drivers in the house each have a car, or when there is enough money in your wallet for gasoline.

Our financial situation just prior to Tayler's birth was not the greatest. Kara's medical bills were astronomical, and our insurance did not cover everything. Still, we felt like we had a handle on it all.

We were in the process of buying a town house that Brad would fix up for our expanding family. And just when we needed some stability in our lives, our second car, which had been threatening to die, did so. We did not have the money to bring it back to life, let alone buy another car. That was okay though, because I could schedule Kara's doctor appointments around Brad's work hours. I would be home for the most part anyway with the new baby. It sounded like it would all work out. We were not concerned about getting from A to B.

Then Tayler came into the picture. One of the first things that her general surgeon said after her first surgery was that if she lived through this at all, she would be in the ICU for at least five months. *Five months!* Once we digested that shocking news, we started to create our plan of transportation to make it all work.

Kara was bussed to school ten miles south of our home, and the hospital was twenty miles north. The RTD (Rapid Transit District) was looking like the extra car for us. Eventually Brad would have to return to work and leave me without a car.

Visiting Tayler every day after I had sent Kara off to school and to therapy was never a problem. I didn't even have to make a phone call. One friend after another would offer their car for me to use. Sometimes friends would give me a ride themselves. Others would lend their car for a day, two days, sometimes even a week.

All the while, Brad and I were learning that insurance would not be paying for all of Tayler's hospital stay. We thought we were doomed. Not only were the dreams of having any healthy children in our family shattered, but we were also on our way to financial ruin.

In the background, Sandy and Stephen and Scott and Darla were heading up a group effort among our other friends to do the most incredible deed that we had ever heard.

In Tayler's third month in the hospital, several of our amazing friends invited us to have Sunday brunch in a restaurant in Laguna Beach. We were feeling loved and cared for by some of the most supportive people we would ever know. At the end of the meal, the time came for us to make the trip up to the hospital and spend the rest of the day with Tayler.

The whole group followed us out to the parking structure to see us off. Then while we were walking to the car, Scott handed Brad a set of keys. He pointed to a beautiful gray car with a huge pink bow on top of it. And with everyone's eyes on us he said, "These car keys are for you, and that car with the bow on it is yours too."

You can imagine the instant tears that flowed—not just from our eyes, but from everyone's. The act of giving gave them a sense of complete satisfaction. They knew our need and went to great lengths to fill that need for us. In the front seat of the car was a big box full of comfortable clothing made by Sandy's sportswear company, and the card that summed it all up simply said,

"Through your friends, Love, Jesus"

Without our knowledge, twenty-nine people contributed to that outstanding gift. Years later, Stephen said to me that giving that car to us was one of the highlights of his life. And I believe him.

We couldn't wait for our chance to do such a deed for someone else. Many years later, we were close friends to a family in a similar situation. Brad and I looked at each other and I said, "Let's get on the phone." Within weeks, one of our mutual friends had suggested that she donate her unneeded second car to a church, and in turn the church passed it on to the family. The family was just as astounded by such a huge gift as we had been.

It truly was a great pleasure to give, or to help someone who had the means to give channel her gift to someone who greatly needed it. Giving a car or being part of the process was quite an experience.

THOUGHTFUL SUGGESTIONS

1. Lend your time to transport someone to a necessary destination.
2. Lend your car during a time when you don't personally need it for a few hours or a day or however long you can. Don't wait for your friends to ask for your help. Just call them and offer what you can.
3. Lend your friends an extra car if you have one.
4. Research ways in which to purchase a car, or if appropriate, a motorcycle or maybe even a bicycle. Call mutual friends to see if they have an extra car that they would like to donate if you don't have one yourself. Contact a church or tax-exempt organization to collaborate with. Dealerships in your area may be interested in helping out when you tell them of the reason for the need.
5. If long-term help is needed and the only means of commuting will have to be the local transportation system, then assist the person by calling the transit districts and asking for the routing information, running times, and cost.
6. There are situations when air transportation is needed, maybe even an emergency flight. Some airlines, though not all, are willing to reduce their fees in such cases. Rally people together to help in whatever ways they can.
7. Donate your frequent flier miles to a friend in need.

Giving something as magnificent as a car seems like an overwhelming task. It definitely takes research, solicitation, and time. If a car is the right thing to give to someone, it won't be out of reach.

Assisting a person or family in need of transportation will be appreciated beyond belief. Trust me, we know. Keep this in mind when you ask your friend or loved one, "How can I help you?"

> LORD, you have searched me
>   and you know me.
> You know when I sit and when I rise;
>   you perceive my thoughts from afar.
> You discern my going out and my lying down;
>   you are familiar with all my ways.
> Before a word is on my tongue
>   you know it completely, O LORD.

> Psalm 139:1–4

26

PARTY IT UP!

Kara was five years old and Tayler was one year old when I was barely pregnant with our third baby. We had been attending Saddleback Valley Community Church in our area, and they welcomed our Kara in their classrooms with open arms. That's where I first met Debbie. She worked as a leader in the children's program and bonded with Kara right away. I'll never forget the way she tried to assist me at church in every way that she could with the girls, even helping me to the car when Brad couldn't join us because he had to work.

Fast approaching was the summer of 1990, just a few short weeks before Paige would be born. Though I hadn't known Debbie for long, she asked me if she could give me a baby shower for my new little one. I said, "Thank you, but I don't plan on having a shower for my third child, and besides I don't want to bother any of my friends for a gift." She said that she wasn't planning on inviting my friends, but that she was inviting all of her friends. I didn't quite understand. She said to just leave it up to her and let her do this for me. Knowing Debbie as I do now, it was just as much fun for her to plan this wonderful party as it was for me to be the recipient.

As I recall, there were approximately twenty women at the shower, including Brad's mother and my sister-in-law, Renee. I was amazed. When each of the ladies introduced herself, almost without fail she would say, "If you're a friend of Debbie's, you're a friend of mine." Wow! What a compliment to Deb.

The gifts were as generous as each one of those women. Then just after the last gift was opened, and I gave what I thought was the final thank-you to all, Debbie announced that there was one more gift, and she instructed me to turn around and look behind me. She had constructed a money tree with actual money on it. The women that Debbie had invited to the shower who couldn't attend, as well as those who had already given me a gift, contributed to this tree. These women, because of Debbie's faithful friendship to them, produced nearly three hundred dollars for our family.

Debbie gladly threw a party for someone whom she barely knew. That act of love from her and from each woman who supported her will always be an amazing memory.

For some people and for certain situations, a party is most inappropriate. Long-term illness or depression should be dealt with gingerly. *No surprises* unless they have hinted that they have never been given a surprise party before and have said that it is something they've always wanted. Be a student of the person in your life who is or has been hurting. Being too cheerful may seem like you are unsympathetic in regard to her pain. Your goal here is to help. "Life is a party" only when you are able to

THOUGHTFUL SUGGESTIONS

1. Rally together friends of the person or family that is hurting. Let them know that you are giving them a barbeque at your home. If the family or person is not able to come to you, then go to them. Give them some lead time to prepare for company. Bring streamers, balloons, the whole ball of wax. All of this after asking permission, of course.
2. Hang a "Welcome Home" banner on the garage door or in the front of their home for their arrival from the hospital. Balloons make it even more festive. This may be all the party atmosphere the family can handle at this time.
3. Call ahead to the hospital to let them know that you and a few friends will be stopping by for a visit. Bring a boom box and party hats. Quietly play something that they would enjoy. Don't forget that this person may have a sleeping roommate.
4. Dress up as an animal (call yourself the party animal) and show up at their doorstep. They will think you are absolutely crazy and will love you for bringing a little laughter into their life. Rental costume shops are in the Yellow Pages. Look one up.

enjoy it. Gently bring a party to your loved one or friend. Two people can make a party just as easily as a roomful can.

Therefore, since we are surrounded by such a great cloud of witnesses, let us throw off everything that hinders and the sin that so easily entangles, and let us run with perseverance the race marked out for us. Let us fix our eyes on Jesus, the author and perfecter of our faith, who for the joy set before him endured the cross, scorning its shame, and sat down at the right hand of the throne of God.

Hebrews 12:1–2

27

WHO WROTE THE BOOK
OF LOVE?

I met my friend Andi when we cochaired the PTA presidency for our children's school. She has three children, Danny, Jeremy, and Missy. Jeremy and Missy were enrolled at R. H. Dana Exceptional Needs Facility, and so was my Kara. I was attracted to Andi's undying sense of humor amidst her family's situation. She is a giver and always makes you feel like a million dollars when you walk into a room.

She joined me in the hospital when Kara needed a spinal tap to test for spinal meningitis. She and her husband, Richard, were among our friends who joined us in the waiting room while Tayler was undergoing her first major surgery. She was one of the first persons to welcome Paige into the world. Andi has been there through it all, and she has supported me in ways that would take another volume to explain.

Her oldest son, Jeremy, was diagnosed with cerebral palsy when he was two years old and Andi was pregnant with twins, Danny and Missy. When the twins were born, Missy was almost immediately diagnosed with cerebral palsy also. Danny was perfectly healthy. Andi and Richard weathered many storms with the raising of their three children, and they did it with much patience and grace.

Andi never dwells on her own circumstances, which makes her a hero in my mind. She is always one to put out a fire for another who is hurting.

In January 2000 they were faced with a tragic fire of their own. A faulty wire in a lightbulb in their garage became hazardous. Without warning, it sparked, caught on fire, and caused a major blaze that destroyed their cars and the left wing of their home and caused smoke damage to most of their belongings. Fortunately no one was hurt, but it was devastating just the same. They lived in hotels for about a month, awaiting the availability of a home to rent while their house was being rebuilt. The contractors said that it would take at least six months to reconstruct their home.

Struggling to know what to do for them, I thought about my own children and what they could do first. I wanted them to write a note to Jeremy, Missy, and Danny. But then I thought that maybe my children's classmates could write a note too, and draw a picture to show their kindness and caring for someone they knew only through Kara, Tayler, and Paige. That's just what they did. Each child in the girls' classrooms wrote a note and drew a picture for the family. The notes were precious. The teachers were so gracious about the added classroom time

THOUGHTFUL SUGGESTIONS

1. Combine a gallery of poems. Bind them in any way you like. Be creative and make it as professional looking as you can. Include your own thoughts or write a poem of your own for your hurting friend.
2. Put together a small book of inspirational Bible verses. Use your best handwriting or calligraphy and some pretty paper or stationery.
3. Compose your own small book. Let it be a short story, either fact or fiction. Your friend will love you for making the effort to express your friendship in a genuine and unique way using your own words. Staple the edge of the pages and glue attractive buttons over the staples to dress it up a little.

it took to do this task. I gathered all of the notes, about sixty of them, placed each one in a plastic protective sleeve, and then bound them in a nice three-ringed binder. I had a hard time choosing the picture that became the cover of the book. They were all masterpieces.

Robin, another friend of Andi's, had a similar idea. She gathered notes from Andi and Richard's gallery of friends and family. The following was my family's somewhat lighthearted, hopefully heartwarming letter that expressed our love for the Mandel family.

May 7, 2000

Dear Richard, Andi, Jeremy, Danny, and Missy,
We are constantly ablaze, we mean amazed, at the way you all seem to get people's attention. God must have a real burning, we mean yearning, to show you how very much he loves you.

So many lives have been torched, we mean touched, by the way that you keep your sense of humor through it all. There is no possible way that we can exhaust, we mean express, how much we admire you for the ways that you continue to put out fires, we mean pour out kindness, of spirit and generosity even still. We are ignited by your friendship and we know that the bomb, we mean bond, that we share will stay kindled forever.

We love you, Brad, Terri, Kara, Tayler, and Paige

Including other people when creating a thoughtful gesture for your hurting friend or loved one gives supporters of the family a chance to feel useful. Call a group you are involved with, maybe of longtime friends, co-workers, church family, or even just your family and extended family members, who would be willing to join you in your efforts.

Who wrote the book of love? I would say billions of thoughtful people who put together in words an expression of caring and understanding throughout the years. The readings have different words, but the message is still the same: "I care about you and this is my expression of love."

He [Jahaziel, a Levite] said: "Listen, King Jehoshaphat and all who live in Judah and Jerusalem! This is what the LORD says to you: 'Do not be afraid or discouraged because of this vast army. For the battle is not yours, but God's.'"

2 Chronicles 20:15

28

PLEASE WASH ME

Brad and I were married on the first day of summer, June 21, 1980. It was a bright sunny week before the wedding, and everything was fitting into place. It was a bittersweet time for us though. My father had passed away just nine weeks before. He had asked me to choose his birthday for our wedding date, but it was on a Wednesday, so we decided it would be best to set it for the Saturday before. He asked that I not replace him for my walk down the aisle if he could not be present at my wedding. There was no question but that I would honor his request. And the moment that the wedding march began, I could feel the spirit of his presence by my side. The photograph of me that captures that moment shows a bride at perfect peace with the world. I knew that my father loved Brad and that he would have been proud to walk me down the aisle and give me away to him.

Linda was one of my bridesmaids. She was also my roommate for several months while my father was going through his illness. She had done many things for me. She offered to do anything that I needed, from running pre-wedding errands to cleaning my apartment. However, she was a single parent and I didn't want her to go to any trouble.

Brad and I were driving up to Lake Tahoe for our honeymoon in my light yellow Camaro with a white interior. It was filthy. Linda showed up just a couple of days ahead with a bucket and a sponge to clean our lemon yellow limo. What a thoughtful friend. Linda always wanted to cheer up the hurting and help out a busy friend.

Brad and I made the trip north to Lake Tahoe for our honeymoon and drove back home down the coast. It was a beautiful

THOUGHTFUL SUGGESTIONS

1. There are so many tasks to do around a home. When people are mentally or physically hurting, things just don't get done. Take a squeegee and some towels, some soap and a hose, and just show up on your friends' doorstep. Tell them that the cleaning crew is here to do outdoor household chores.
2. Wash their car. Put a note on the driver's seat after you've completed the job that says, "We are here for you and we are willing to help out in any way that we can."
3. Wash their windows. Got a tall ladder? If not, borrow one. It can be a great surprise to look out of the house through sparkling clean windows and screens.
4. Clean the garage door and the front door. Hose down their hardscape in the front and in the back.
5. Clean out their rain gutters.
6. Clean and polish a child's bike or a wheelchair.

drive and our car was sparkling clean thanks to our dear friend. The end of the story isn't as pretty though. We stopped in front of Brad's parents' home before we went to our apartment for the very first time. While we were visiting with them, the transmission slipped out of our car and onto the street in front of their house where we had parked. (A suggestion for the mechanically inclined friend might be to offer to inspect a good pal's car before a long trip. That's another deed for another chapter.)

As for cleanliness, it must be next to godliness. At least we made it home from our honeymoon journey, and we weren't stranded on the highway with dirt covering our car and the words "PLEASE WASH ME" etched in the dust over the "JUST MARRIED" sign. Thank you again, Linda.

Let us not become weary in doing good, for at the proper time we will reap a harvest if we do not give up.

Galatians 6:9

29

LET IT SNOW

We've all seen the canisters or money tins in the super-markets. You know, the ones with the labels on the front that request a donation for a specific charity. There are the Easter Seals, the United Cerebral Palsy Organization, and the Fight for Muscular Dystrophy, to name just a few. I always wondered what these associations really did with the money they collect. Is the money raised only for research? Or do they really help people who have the disability that they represent? Now that we've become a recipient family of the benefits of some of these organizations, I've been allowed the privilege to find out.

All three of our girls were very young when we were invited to an Easter luncheon that was held at the Disneyland Hotel by the Easter Seals organization. The presentation and atmosphere were absolutely beautiful. All of the families who were invited had children with various disabilities. It was a gorgeous sunny day, and the hotel was magnificently decorated. The Easter Bunny was in his Sunday best, and he sat ready for the next little one in line to take the annual picture on his lap.

I don't recall any speeches being given that day and there was

THOUGHTFUL SUGGESTIONS

1. Let's say that you live nowhere near the beach, but it's hot outside. A cool splash of waves would sure put out the physical and emotional fire for a while. Young and old alike, everyone loves a little imagination. Find a local pool that you can use to throw a beach blanket shindig. You can buy sand at any local hardware store. Decorate a bank off of the pool area with a Kona shack, tiki lamps, and seashells for a nonliving crustacean hunt. Find plastic sharks and sea animals that can float in the pool. Be sure to have beach balls to bounce everywhere and a large fish net to catch stray people—I mean fish. Music sets the scene just right with the Beach Boys or Honk. A little Beach Blanket Bingo music and a few Gidget tunes would add an extra touch. Burgers and hot dogs are inexpensive cuisine. Ice-cream bars dipped in chocolate are a favorite in our local town of Balboa, but homemade ice cream would really take the cake.

2. It's really cold out there. It's so cold that it's sure to snow any minute now, but even if it never does, there are snow machines to rent that really do the trick. Some kids with medical complications may never be able to go to the mountains or use a snow sled. How about bringing the mountains to them? Find a park near their home that has a slope just steep enough to get a little speed behind a snow dish with the child and attendant on it. If you tell the snow machine company the reason for the rental, they may be willing to donate a large portion of the equipment costs for your hours of use. It never hurts to ask.

nothing sold or solicited. It was strictly a day for families to feel appreciated and celebrated for merely hanging in there for the long haul and for making it through the good and bad times.

The following winter our family was invited to a snow day in the park, which the Easter Seals also sponsored. As I recall, it hadn't snowed for years in the town where this creative activity took place. But that didn't stop this determined group of many volunteers and employees. There were snow machines set up everywhere. There were small slopes in this park that made for great toboggan trips. They had roped off areas for safety so that little ones couldn't get off the beaten snow path. It was a great day full of fantasy winter wonderland, complete with a roaming Ronald McDonald and Disneyland characters. Lunch was catered free by fast-food establishments from all over the city. The vendors who donated their time, services, and fun party items seemed endless.

This is not Candid Camera, but don't be surprised if someone, somewhere, when you least expect it, is planning a day of wonder and excitement for you. Help that friend out with a hint, a wish list of what you would really like to do if you could just get out of the house for the day, get out of that wheelchair, or get that dumb cast off. Most of us appreciate surprises, but even better, we all just want to be thought of and loved.

Come to me, all you who are weary and burdened, and I will give you rest. Take my yoke upon you and learn from me, for I am gentle and humble in heart, and you will find rest for your souls. For my yoke is easy and my burden is light.

Matthew 11:28–30

30

DRIVE 'EM WILD

Fund-raising is one of my favorite things to do. When you know there is a need that must be filled, and without the help of many volunteers the financial assistance just won't be there, it's time for a paper drive of sorts.

Being the co-president of the PTA at Kara's school, I was automatically given the responsibility to raise funds for the children's extracurricular activities. I was overwhelmed by the number of willing participants who were happy to give to these adorable children with disabilities. The funds provided these kids with the opportunity to see what the typical child sees. The results might fund a field trip to the zoo or a whale-watching expedition along the coast of the Pacific Ocean. Many other ways to further the experiences of these children who had a need for assistance were made possible because of people with unselfish hearts.

One of our fund-raising efforts was for two beneficiaries: R. H. Dana Exceptional Needs School and the world-renowned Special Olympics. Living in Southern California gave me interesting opportunities to raise funds.

Pilar Wayne was a resident of Newport Beach. She was a former movie star and the wife of the "Duke," John Wayne. She shared the same hair stylist as a friend of Andi's, so that's how the ball started rolling. Pilar offered her home as the setting for the benefit. She jokingly called it a Hollywood Party.

Pilar became interested in helping children who had joined the Special Olympics, and she asked what she should say on that evening to welcome the guests to her home. Brad knew just what she should say, and he also gave her a Bible verse to quote, Isaiah 40:31.

"All of these children who will benefit from this evening's proceeds are hindered in their athletic abilities. But the fact is children with disabilities are also children of God, and while they are here on this earth they have a different purpose than most," Pilar told the evening's guests. "When they reach heaven, the Bible is clear as to their future: 'Those who hope in the LORD will renew their strength. They will soar on wings like eagles; they will run and not grow weary, they will walk and not be faint.'"

Everyone's time is valuable. Being a part of bringing people together for a common goal is so rewarding in the end. Not everything will always run smoothly, but keep in mind the whole motivation behind your efforts. There is a child who needs a reason to smile. There is a wheelchair needed, a set of crutches, financial assistance for an operation, or a day of respite for a caretaker. The needs are endless. Don't sit back in that living-room recliner forever—simply pitch in.

THOUGHTFUL SUGGESTIONS

1. Plan a fashion show like we did on the tennis courts of Pilar's home. Be sure to have someone in charge of each aspect of the event. The invitations, the food, the decorations, the facility, and in this case, the stage and seating, are just a few of the areas that need one person in charge. The lighting, the models, the designer, the hair stylist, the thank-yous, the cleanup and takedown are also important to delegate. Don't leave one stone unturned. Be assured that a huge function like this will take your life away as you know it for the duration of its preparation, the event itself, and the follow-up. Let your husband (or wife) know that your marriage will be on hold, and ask him (or her) if he would be a single parent to your children while this is all taking place.

2. Have a simple car wash or a pizza night at the local pizzeria. Many restaurants are willing to share the profits when raising money for a special project.

3. Call the media. Write and send a fax to all the local radio stations and newspapers. Let them know of the need and let the community be a part of the giving.

4. Sell lemonade, pastries, baked goods, fresh donuts, muffins, pies, and cans of soda. Work with the local bakeries and grocery stores for donated items. Ask the volunteers of this fund-raiser to bake their favorites for the worthwhile cause.

5. Most of the businesses that donate their services need a letter of request that includes a tax I.D. number. You may not already have a tax-exempt organization set up. That process is time consuming and can take up to six months. It takes paperwork and an application to the IRS, so plan ahead if you can. If you can work through a school, a club, or an association that would be willing to join you in your fund-raising efforts, you may be able to avoid the application process altogether. However, each organization has its own set of bylines that govern the reason for their legally obtained tax-exempt status. Your fund-raiser must meet the organization's guidelines.

Do what you can to help someone who needs you. You will be glad you did.

> Never tire of doing what is right.
>
> 2 Thessalonians 3:13

31

MOLLY MAID

I t was brought to my attention that the local United Cerebral Palsy Association was hiring a parent of children with disabilities to coordinate a program called Parent Connection. It is a collaborative effort of UCP and The Family Resource Center for parents of children with disabilities.

Eventually I was hired to coordinate the South Orange County English-speaking parent volunteers of children with disabilities. We had a volunteer pool of about 175 parents who were willing to talk on the phone for emotional support or share resources with another parent of a child with the same or similar disability. All the parents were gracious and eager to communicate positive experiences and resources that worked for them and their child in regard to their therapies, medical attention, or community involvement. Many times a mother or father would clearly need a sympathetic, listening ear to share his or her own hurts and frustrations about being the parent of a child with disabilities.

Sometimes the volunteers would go beyond the call of duty. One particular parent in need was a single mom of a child with reflux, a condition that usually rights itself with maturity but drives most mothers to tears in the meantime. Reflux is simply the inability to keep food contained within the stomach. It is a regurgitation that occurs because of a malfunction of an immature valve in the child's esophagus.

This mother was struggling to cope with her premature infant and his inability to keep food down. Her home had gone without attention, and she was simply unable to get to the supermarket. She was in a financial crisis as well.

I shared this case with my friend Renee, a volunteer for the program, and some other friends from church. They all agreed that we should simply show up and clean this woman's home, bring food for her, and run errands that she could not manage on her own. It was a knee-jerk reaction resulting in many kind deeds done for this woman that my friends had never met.

One day we took cleansers, buckets, brooms, and just about everything we needed to do a major overhaul to this mother's two-bedroom home. To add to her troubles, her leg was also broken. She could not get upstairs, so she had a bedroom/living room/den and kitchen set up in one room. It was quite a sight. Without much conversation, we all went to work. I recall that it took us hours to complete our mission.

We'd all love it if someone would come alongside us and scrub our floors, clean our windows, and do our other unpleasant household chores when we need help. Sometimes pitching in means doing what needs to be done even if it isn't what we want to do very badly. That's part of the giving!

THOUGHTFUL SUGGESTIONS

1. No doubt you have known or will know of someone who has a need in the housekeeping department at some point. Everyone could use a helping hand now and then. Give your struggling friend or loved one a call to offer your help with laundry, dishwashing, window cleaning, and other chores.
2. Your local church, school, or workplace would be a good source of leads to find out who has this kind of need. Give the church your phone number and volunteer your services at the church's request.
3. Can you grab a handful of friends who would be willing to whistle while they work to make a dusty room smell like sunshine? Maybe you know of a group of Girl Scouts who are looking to earn a domestic badge.

The woman with the baby moved to Florida where she could have continued support from her mother and cousin. Before she left, she never stopped thanking our group of women for pitching in when she couldn't do it herself. I hope that she carries God's love for her wherever she goes. My undying thanks go out to my great friends Remy, Teri, Renee, and many others for their selfless acts of help for this woman in need.

Each one should use whatever gift he has received to serve others, faithfully administering God's grace in its various forms.

1 Peter 4:10

32

A Barn Raising

Paul was one of the most well-liked men at the Newport Beach Police Department. He was kind to everyone he met, and he would do anything he could for someone who needed assistance or even for someone who just needed a little home repair. Paul is a perfectionist. He is a master craftsman. He can make anything with his bare hands, and it looks professionally made.

There was no greater jeopardy for him than working as a police officer until he took one too many falls in the medical world. He contracted cancer in his right leg, which left him needing surgery and other treatment procedures. He wouldn't let that stop him, though, until one day when he rode his bicycle to work and was struck by a car. His left leg was shattered. He was fortunate to be alive.

Struggle after struggle, Paul kept trying to mend and come back to police life. He worked at the front desk for quite some time while he went through the cancer treatments and also while he recovered from the many surgeries necessary after the traffic accident.

What a trooper he was. He would come with his wife, Kim, to a support group of fellow police officers and their wives. Brad and I also attended. Paul would not let anyone spend much time fussing over what he was going through. He would much rather focus on how he could help someone else.

Finally it was Paul's turn to be the focus of others besides Kim. They had bought a home on a piece of horse property many miles inland from most of us, and it needed much repair. Being the handyman, Paul wasn't used to having anyone's help, but he recognized the need for assistance from others this time, and the rest of the guys couldn't wait to do something for him. One weekend, the guys took hammer and nails and went to Paul's aid. They put Paul and Kim's kitchen together in one day. They hung cabinets and sunk countertops. Paul's perfectionism

THOUGHTFUL SUGGESTIONS

1. Possibly you have a neighbor who is up in his years, and he could use a little help with the exterior of his home. Do like the Amish and gather a group of men around you to find how you can help this neighbor.
2. You could head up a group of handymen for your neighborhood. What a great way to bring unity in the place where you live.
3. Do you have a senior community nearby? We do, and I bet they would be incredibly grateful for a group of hardworking men to help out on a project that the homeowner can no longer do himself.

didn't waver. He had those guys doing it right. A quarter of an inch made all the difference to Paul. Remember, he is a master at his craft.

Just writing this chapter gets me excited about starting something like this in my own neighborhood. Brad is great at making our house a structurally sound home. I can just imagine that he would love to rally our neighborhood men together to be available for those on our little cul-de-sac who could use some major or minor repairs on their homes. But never volunteer your man for anything. I've been guilty of that a few too many times. Simply leave a bookmark in this chapter and ask him if he would like to read a story about a cop. Who knows, maybe it will give him an idea of his own.

Paul continued to be a giver, and he and Kim had a barn-raising barbeque to gather their friends as a thank-you for helping them beautifully restore their home. He has since retired on medical leave from the police force, and he has successfully started his own business making knives. We miss our great times together at the police functions, but we will never lose each other's friendship.

Make it your ambition to lead a quiet life, to mind your own business and to work with your hands, just as we told you.

1 Thessalonians 4:11

33

WATTS THE MATTER?

Have you ever been told that you light up someone's life? I mean literally light up someone's life? While Andi and I co-chaired the presidency of the PTA, we had the privilege of knowing which families needed Christmas cheer and how their needs could be met.

One Christmas, she had a great idea. We wanted to bring one special family chosen by the principal of the school some light in their Christmas. We brought multicolored Christmas lights to decorate their tree and tiny white lights for the wreath that we had brought to hang on their front door. We laced lights on pictures that hung on the wall. And then, not to overdo it, on top of the coffee table we wove lights around a nativity set.

Two of the boys in this single mother's family were developmentally disabled. The third boy was an infant and too young to be positively diagnosed, but he was believed to be blind. Lights stimulate the brain and can aid a young one to retain any sight he does have.

The father had abandoned the mother of these three boys. She had been addicted to cigarettes, drugs, and more. These

THOUGHTFUL SUGGESTIONS

1. Do some research to find a family that is in need at Christmastime. Your local elementary schools can help you out here. If you are in a position on the PTA board, this will be much easier to do. The school most likely will not give out names to you, but you can find out specific needs through the faculty.

2. Let's face it; the women of the house generally carry out most of the duties at Christmastime. We do the shopping, wrapping, cooking, cleaning, decorating, party planning, and so on. The men generally come into the picture when it comes to placing the outdoor Christmas lights. The gift to a family of lighting up their home could be right up a man's alley.

3. Give your husband or the man in your life the idea and let him be a bigger part of researching a family in need of some light in their life. Maybe it is a co-worker who has had a difficult time making ends meet because of some financial hardship in the past year.

4. There are colored lights sold now for almost every holiday: lights that form a red, white, and blue flag for the 4th of July; amber lights for harvest time celebrations; a green shamrock on St. Patrick's Day; and a pastel cross on Easter. These are a few suggestions.

5. Slip a check for a sizable amount of money in a Christmas card. That can pay for the electric bill. After all, you don't want your gift to go unused because there are no funds to turn on the lights.

children were innocent victims of the harm adults can bring to themselves and ultimately pass down to their offspring.

We can all hope and pray that a family's trouble is only temporary and that our lights are another way to brighten up the family's holiday season. No one should be without support when they are down. A dark home during the Christmas season can compound the disappointment of the hardships that they are facing.

It's no secret that Jesus is the reason for the season. And what would Jesus do if he were physically sitting next to one of us on Christmas Day? I believe he would whisper in our ear something like, "I am the Light of the World, go and share my light with others."

> The LORD is my light and my salvation—
> whom shall I fear?
> The LORD is the stronghold of my life—
> of whom shall I be afraid?
>
> Psalm 27:1

PART 4

IN CONCLUSION

34

IT'S NEVER TOO LATE

So many times I have heard people say, "Oh, if I had only known about the fund-raiser [or the group gift or helping by volunteering], then I would have given too." That's when you create a new opportunity to help. This is your chance to stand up and be counted. God will help guide you in your efforts to help. With any fund-raising effort I have been involved in, there were always the one or two people who wanted to be a part of it, but the timing just wasn't right. Maybe the timing wasn't right then, but there is always something you can do or say eventually.

The 9-11 attacks on our nation left many of us speechless, helpless, motionless, and tearfully drained for days. Most of the world was horrified and grief stricken. Many of our citizens came to the forefront immediately with immeasurable aid. At times there was even an overabundance of food, supplies, donated blood, and volunteers. It was an amazing outpouring of devotion and commitment to fellow Americans from all over the United States.

Certain celebrities performed in a nationwide telethon to raise monies for the families of the victims of this tragedy. California firefighters who were available and were not shipped out to help at the sites of the devastation were collecting donations in firefighter boots. Lemonade stands were sprouting up everywhere. Flags of every size were being sold on many corners, with vendors sending their profits to the victims. The wait to donate blood to the Red Cross was hours long.

Our emotions were high, and it helped our raw grieving in some small way to give or do something constructive because we couldn't do anything to give back the lives that were taken or fill the void of a lost parent or spouse, brother or sister, child or grandparent. There is no American that has not been affected in some way by all the tragedy and sorrow.

THOUGHTFUL SUGGESTIONS

1. It's never too late to donate blood to the Red Cross. When the blood banks come into a slow period, it doesn't mean that they are not in need of blood to help out all over the country.
2. It's never too late to send money for the nation's relief funds. There is never too much money to help out with a support effort.
3. It's never too late to write a letter to your president to express your support of his strategy to save our country from future disasters like the attacks of 9-11.
4. It will never be too late to send encouraging notes to the men and women who serve our country every day in the daily emergencies, large and small, that happen in every city.

If you didn't do something then for the families, the cities, the president, the business owners, the servicemen, the rescue workers, or the countless other people who could have used encouragement, there are many ways that you still can help.

A letter, a note, supplies, money, phone calls, flowers, food, clothing, shelter, sacrificial giving of any kind, and loving support in every way are all what God intended us to give one another in a crisis, in hardship, in good times, or in bad times.

Hold everything you own with an open hand. For every talent that you have and every minute you have to give, share it with someone who needs you. Reach out even when it is uncomfortable. And know that the more you give, the more your heart will receive.

Do nothing out of selfish ambition or vain conceit, but in humility consider others better than yourselves. Each of you should look not only to your own interests, but also to the interests of others.

Philippians 2:3–4

35

LORD, GIVE ME STRENGTH

I love the song "Turn, Turn, Turn." The original single was recorded by a band called The Byrds. When I listened to it as a child, I had no idea that it was based on the Book of Ecclesiastes in the Bible. The song contains words similar to those in Ecclesiastes 3:1: "There is a time for everything, and a season for every activity under heaven."

It is not necessary to mention the importance of being a full-time mother in my home with our three young girls. There is no need to explain that my husband needed a full-time wife to support him through his dangerous career. But all I could focus on for many years were people that were hurting all around us. I would constantly channel my attention to those who didn't seem to have anyone to help them. I falsely believed that no one else would step in if I didn't help.

I wasn't working my way toward being recognized as the next Mother Teresa (Mother Terri). I was just plugging along outside of my home, trying to fill needs around us regardless of the constant cries from Brad and our girls for me to stay home and help them. I had been given many opportunities to help others in my church and my community. I felt assured that what I was doing was the right thing because it was a good thing.

In 1999 I was given the Volunteer of the Year Award by the State of California for my work with people with disabilities. The beautifully etched glass trophy holds two meanings in our home.

Brad says that he is proud of me and of the work I did for others. He has asked me many times to display the award trophy in our living room. But for me the honor is a reminder that I had no business taking that much time away from my young family to tend to other families' needs in the capacity that I did. I guess I was just in a hurry to give back to others for what so many had done for us for so many years.

I am fortunate that my little family hung in there with me while I was out there trying to extinguish fires that weren't our own. I now realize that I need to put our family first. Finally I am focusing more on their successes and comforting them through their disappointments while they are still young and growing. I also know that Brad is much wiser than I am. He is my barometer. He helps me to give my attention to God and my family first.

My desire to comfort those parents who have children with special needs is still strong. My prayer at this time in my life is that there will be someone else more fitting to come alongside them in their time of great need. As strange as it sounds, I know that I was being selfish by giving to others. It gave me great satisfaction, but my giving was mainly outside of my family.

There is a time and a season for every purpose. I understand that statement clearly now. I do pray that when it is my time again to help others in a big way outside of my family, the Lord will give me the strength to do it. Not just the physical strength, but strength of mind to know when to say enough and to come back home to the ones for whom I truly live my life.

The joy of the Lord is your strength.

Nehemiah 8:10

May God richly bless you for the thoughtfulness that you show to your family and to others. When the season comes for you to prayerfully consider using your time and talents to give outside of meeting your own family's immediate needs, consider this Bible passage:

When you give a banquet, invite the poor, the crippled, the lame, the blind, and you will be blessed. Although they cannot repay you, you will be repaid at the resurrection of the righteous.

Luke 14:13–14

If this book has been an inspiration to you I would love to hear your story. Please contact me by email (info@simple-acts.com) or my website (www.simple-acts.com). Let me know how you have helped someone in your life that has experienced hardship.

Terri Green has been an inspirational speaker for over twelve years. She addresses audiences with her unique story of encouragement. In 1999 she received the Volunteer of the Year Award given by the State of California for her work with people who have developmental disabilities. Motivated by the requirements of her oldest daughter, Kara, who has been diagnosed with severe cerebral palsy, Terri created a program for children with special needs in one of the largest non-denominational congregations in America, Saddleback Valley Community Church.

Terri has chaired various fund-raising committees that have supported numerous organizations devoted to people with developmental delay. She also coordinated a program for the United Cerebral Palsy Association that was designed to provide support for parents of children with special needs. Terri resides in Southern California with her husband, Brad, and their three daughters.